ARTHURIAN LITERATURE

XI

ARTHURIAN LITERATURE

ISSN 0261–9946

The contents of previous volumes are listed at the back of this volume.

Arthurian Literature XI

EDITED BY RICHARD BARBER

Advisory editors

Tony Hunt
Toshiyuki Takamiya

D. S. BREWER

© Contributors 1992

First published 1992 by D. S. Brewer, Cambridge

D. S. Brewer is an imprint of Boydell & Brewer Ltd
PO Box 9, Woodbridge, Suffolk IP12 3DF, UK
and of Boydell & Brewer Inc.
PO Box 41026, Rochester, NY 14604, USA

ISBN 0 85991 350 3

British Library Cataloguing-in-Publication Data
A catalogue record for this series is available
from the British Library

Library of Congress Catalog Card Number: 83–640196

The paper used in this publication meets the minimum requirements
of American National Standard for Information Sciences –
Permanence of Paper for Printed Library Materials, ANSI Z39.48–1984

Printed in Great Britain by
St Edmundsbury Press Ltd, Bury St Edmunds, Suffolk

CONTENTS

EDITOR'S PREFACE

As from volume XII, the editorship of *Arthurian Literature* will be taken over by Dr James Carley of the University of York, Toronto, and Professor Felicity Riddy, of Centre for Medieval Studies, University of York. They will welcome offers of suitable papers: as in the past, preference will be given to long articles, of 20,000 words or more in length.

In Quest of Jessie Weston by Janet Grayson, which appears in the present volume, was originally to have been published in the *Studies in Medievalism: Monographs and Texts* series. Its companion volume, *The Romance of Perlesvaus* by Jessie Weston also edited by Janet Grayson, is published in that series, and is available from Boydell & Brewer Ltd.

I

IN QUEST OF JESSIE WESTON

Janet Grayson

Acknowledgement

Several years ago it occurred to me that a biographical tribute to Jessie Weston was in order. She died in September 1928; it seemed appropriate that the world should be reminded of her contribution to Arthurian studies by learning something of her life. But outside of a brief entry in *Who Was Who* giving her date of birth and death, a few book titles, the name of her club (Lyceum), and her London address, nothing was to be gleaned from the usual sources. The DNB never heard of her. *The Times* of London obituary provided essential information of honorary awards and cities where she had attended schools, but as no records dating back a hundred years survived, details were not to be had. Scores of letters went out to libraries and archivists, publishers, university and municipal offices, and to individuals in England and the United States as well who might have knowledge of the whereabouts of literary remains or letters or personal recollections of those who had known her. Word from the many people whom I had contacted (including the legatee of Weston's niece to whom her papers had been passed) – from the secretary of the Salters' Company, the guild to which the Westons have belonged for over a century, to family members who supplied details of family history – led me to conclude, reluctantly, that papers she had left no longer existed.

There was some correspondence in the Houghton Mifflin collection of the Houghton Library at Harvard – an encouraging bundle of "chatty" business letters covering the years of World War I. These surfaced relatively early in my search, raising hopes that there would be other such collections containing details of her active, outgoing life. She was evidently a tireless letter writer in the days when telephones were merely tolerated and a part of the day was set aside for correspondence. Records of the David Nutt Company, her major publisher, had burned in a warehouse fire; and

1

later when Mrs Nutt sold the company to George Bell & Sons, the remaining files were carted off also to be burned. The last group of letters came from the Cambridge University Press, publishers of *From Ritual to Romance*. Among them were comments by T. S. Eliot about a re-issue.

There is no need to belabour the disappointment of having followed every clue and exhausted invention. Weston had lived seventy-eight years; more than fifty years after her death she was still being cited, quoted, and corrected both by admirers and the not-so-admiring. The name Jessie L. Weston (she always used her middle initial) was known even to those who knew little about her books. She lived for her work; there was no reason to think ahead to a future time when her life apart from her scholarship might be of interest to others. She did not leave behind memoirs or literary essays in the manner of contemporaries Jane Harrison and Gilbert Murray. Nor had she an academic circle to keep her name alive in lecture series or memorials. Her dedication to the comparative method that had captivated scholars of her day taught her only too well that nothing was fixed, everything gave way to a next phase. Her life was of value to others insofar as her ideas of origins of medieval romance survived. To be buried in a "perishable coffin" was her last wish; it stands as a judgement of history as well as her life's story. A sad irony, it seemed to me, was the neglect of the journals to which she was a regular contributor to give news of her death more than a few lines of copy. *Romania* hardly noticed.

I am grateful to all who replied to my letters and offered encouragement and suggestions. Many took the trouble to examine municipal and family records, library and museum archives. Special thanks to the National Library of Wales for permission to use the Weston notebooks containing the study of *Perlesvaus* and to Mr P. W. Davies for his research on my behalf; to Mr David Weston and Mr John Weston, both of whom provided details of Weston family history; to Sir Charles Trinder for his suggestions; to the Houghton Library for providing copies of Weston-Houghton-Mifflin correspondence; to Mr Mark Sexton of the New York office of the Cambridge University Press for his help in obtaining the files on *From Ritual to Romance*; and to the research librarians of Keene State College, who located many books for me.

IN QUEST OF JESSIE WESTON

I

It might be said of Jessie Laidlay Weston that like Athena she came fully grown out of the head of the god. When she first burst upon the world of Arthurian studies she was a mature forty years, prepared to challenge the received Word, then dictated by the German and French "inventionist" critics, and soon to make a reputation as England's leading Arthurian scholar, a title modestly worn and vigorously defended until her death in 1928. She died just as she was completing a study of the Old French romance *Perlesvaus*; by then she had to her credit at least twenty books and dozens of articles, including all twelve entries on Arthurian topics in the celebrated eleventh edition of the Encyclopaedia Britannica, and a major piece on the cyclic romances in the Cambridge Mediaeval History.

There were other women in medieval studies: Lucy Paton on fairy mythology, Gertrude Schoepperle on Tristan, Hope Emily Allen and Evelyn Underhill on the mystics, to name the most prominent. But none of these distinguished scholars was so continually embroiled in controversy or courted it so openly, and none was so prolific or energetic a writer as Jessie Weston. Of no other can it be said her star rose and fell and rose again so dramatically. While she lived, she was the redoubtable Miss Weston: strong-willed, independent, indefatigable, inimitable.

Among her friends were the celebrated scholars of the century: W. P. Ker, W. W. Greg, Walter Raleigh; the French Ferdinand Lot, Joseph Bédier, and her mentor Gaston Paris; Celticists Alfred Nutt, John Rhys, the young Roger Sherman Loomis; anthropologist Sir James Frazer and classicist Jane Harrison. She was much admired in America; her books were standard words in many major colleges and universities here.[1] A tireless worker, she claimed always a willingness "to profit from intelligent criticism," but seldom found sufficient cause to change an opinion, no matter how painstaking the arguments presented by her opponents, the lesser of whom she thought pedantic or ignorant, the greater reactionary or hide-bound. *The Times* of London obituary spoke of her "strong and charming personality and her great sense of humor [that] won her the enduring affection of a host of friends all over the world." She was a generous, enthusiastic teacher and friend, welcoming to her home in

---

[1] Inspired by Weston's *Chief Medieval Poets* (1914), Miss Shackford's class at Wellesley sent her a set of their own translations.

London or Paris the young student just beginning a career or the established scholar come to call on "JLW" to share a light tea and Grail talk.
That strong personality noted by the Times strengthened her determination to be heard over the voices of the opposition; it insulated her against
criticism, sometimes mean, sometimes quite reasonable when critics
questioned the evidence she brought forth in support of her theories. In
any event, she led an extremely active social and intellectual life. She was
an early supporter of the *Wagner-verein*, helped found the London
Lyceum, a women's club, in 1904, and from 1897 regularly attended
meetings of the Folk-Lore Society. 1897 was also the year in which her
first publication in the Celtic origins of Arthurian romance appeared. She
lived well, maintained several residences, spent her English holidays in
Bournemouth at the family home "Banavie," and when she was not
travelling across Europe, passed the remaining time in Paris.

Jessie Weston was European-educated, a financially independent spinster, supported in the main by an inheritance from her father and to a
small extent by royalties.[2] But of her first forty years little is known. She
was born in London in December of 1850 to William Weston, prosperous
tea broker and member of the Salters' Company, and his second wife,
Sarah Burton. Jessie, named for the first Mrs Weston, Jessica Laidlay,
daughter of a Scots laird, was the first of three daughters born to Sarah,
who died when the children were very young, Jessie a mere six or seven.
William then married for a third time. Clara King Weston bore five children. How those early years were spent in a well-to-do Victorian household
filled with ten children (seven of them half-sisters and brothers) can be
inferred from what is known of Victorian middle-class life generally. It
became evident early on that Jessie's special gifts should have every
opportunity of development. She was sent first to school in Brighton
where the family had a home, then to Hildesheim, a Hanoverian city
famous for its antiquities, churches, and conservatory.[3] Later she took

---

[2] She kept close scrutiny of her earnings down to the penny, continually objecting to changes in final copy that might be charged against future royalties.
But she was eager to supply friends, family, and colleagues with copies of her
books as they were issued: Singer in Bavaria, Brugger (in and out of Davos –
at death's door, but destined to outlive her), Lot and Bédier in Paris (Bédier
who could not review because he did not want to hurt any one's feelings), her
nephew the Very Reverend Frank Weston, Bishop of Zanzibar ("the most
talked about man in England today" for his controversial stand on church
policy). Even her business letters reveal her extroverted personality.

[3] Her first published work was a long romantic poem of sacrifice and denial
based on the legend of the rose tree in the chancel of the Cathedral of
Hildesheim. Christina Rossetti was a favourite poet.

classes at the Crystal Palace School of Art and studied under Gaston Paris in Paris. War, fire, and time's neglect have blotted out all records of her studies; but clearly her continental training prepared her not only for the demands of the scholar's life, but also for independence of movement and judgement that were exceptional if not unique in her day.

Two decades earlier the overriding duty of a Jessie Weston would have been to home and family, the spinster daughter caring for the widowed father and whatever younger sisters and brothers remained, the girls to be prepared for marriage and the chosen sons groomed to take over the family business or the business of Empire. That she was living with her father at Sydenhall Hill (in Kent, now London) is indicated by her signature on William's death certificate, though she may have been called from France during his last illness. She was then nearly forty. In the 1880s and 90s most women of similar background were destined to marry and raise children; or if they remained spinsters, did charity work among the poor and the sick; if moved by conviction or zeal, they gave themselves to women's causes – the suffrage movement or founding women's clubs largely modelled after the popular literary societies run by men. Until this time on the surface at least Jessie Weston's life promised to follow the pattern set by countless other middle-class maidens – with a crucial difference in her case. When her natural gifts for language and drawing were recognized, it was decided that the usual schedule of polite education at home would not do; her talents should be nourished by schooling abroad. Determination and self-control evident later in her professional relationships were instilled with the loosening of family ties during her early years spent in Germany and France. France especially had always been more tolerant than England of independent, assertive women. Presumably, after 1887 with a good portion of her father's estate settled upon her, she resumed her travels on the continent. With Paris her European home she made herself known to the most important French and German scholars and visited the great libraries for a look at texts at a time when there were practically no printed editions or translations of romances available. Later, the mature Weston was far more comfortably the Englishwoman living year round in Paris, her home, travelling regularly to Germany, Italy, Switzerland, with visits to her family in Brighton and London usually in the late spring or summer.

Yet there was no damage to family traditions left behind. She was the obedient daughter loyal to her family, particularly her full sisters and later her nieces (to whom she willed her entire estate). Growing up in a household bulging with children created the warm, outgoing Aunt Jessie, gave her a zest for friendships and family, and made her staunchly loyal to both. She was always sure of herself, fairly confident of shaping her place in the scheme of things – in those days widening for the ambitious,

5

forceful woman. Marriage, had the prospect ever arisen, would have ended the career she set herself to perfect, for she would have had to give up the most important strength after financial independence, personal independence, freedom of movement. There were many satisfying friendships with both men and women; the young Jessie found much to admire in Gaston Paris and the older Jessie in her friend and mentor Alfred Nutt. These men particularly, embodiments of the twin obsessions of Arthurian and folklore studies, at whose feet she could sit as the adoring pupil, stand out as the centrepieces of her professional life. This is revealed by the elaborate compliments she pays and the heated defence of her teachers against critics and detractors. In her old age, when she had become a celebrity and was herself admired and adored by the young, Mary Williams became a friend, the bond being the closest one next to blood: similar views of Grail origins. She was loyal, whether to a person or an idea.

We are not asked to look into the lives of William Weston, his three wives and ten children (all but Jessie married), to explain her choices. They were probably thrust upon her by the times and in consideration of her superior talents; these were not to be stifled by self-sacrifice ending finally in a patient tolerance of Jessie the kindly maiden aunt. A disciplined woman who had made her way to the top despite the frowning countenance of her time and place towards women with decided views, she was unplagued by paradoxes emotional and filial that worried others. Her enthusiasm was strong, her tastes in romance clear cut from the beginning; she never was embarrassed by her affection for medieval literature or her distaste for the pervasive Romanism. She remained curious about psychic phenomena to the end of her life without the involvement in occult circles she is often charged with, but in conscience and practice followed a rational religion deeply rooted in Old Testament law. In scholarship she was ambitious not merely to be equal, but to be first; and when after 1910 she became the leading English folklorist she stubbornly held to her pre-eminence against powerful challenges. Her scholarship was creative, but not especially original. The theories she developed and popularized sometimes were rooted in other scholars' labors, a fact she readily acknowledged. Seldom did she deny credit where it was due and often wished others would do the same. She delighted in naming her sources old or new, in citing a text whether to compliment or (more often) criticise the favourite shibboleths of others, in commenting on a conversation between herself and this scholar or that – delighted in bringing all members of the Arthurian company into the inimitable circle where they could show their mettle.

It was not until 1892 that she decided on a career that would bring her before the public. The stimulus was Wagner fever, then sweeping across

Europe out of Bayreuth; the occasion, a performance of *Parsifal* aat Bayreuth which she attended with Alfred Nutt. Regretting how little the English knew of the legends behind Wagner's operas, she took up immediately Nutt's suggestion that she make Wagner's sources better known to the public. He would publish. Two years later in 1894 her first book appeared: a verse translation of 2,400 lines in two volumes of Wolfram's *Parzival*, copiously annotated by her with additional notes by Alfred Nutt. This was to remain her personal favourite among her works.[4]

More Weston books followed soon after from the David Nutt press: studies of the *Volsungasaga* and *Nibelungenlied*, then *The Legend of Sir Gawain*, in which she came down firmly for Celtic origins of romance. A book a year, sometimes two, aimed at different audiences poured forth. There seemed to be no stopping the Weston tide. There were books to satisfy the hunger for Germanic legend, Arthurian books for the layman and Arthurian studies for the specialist. Also for the cultivated reader there appeared an edition of her poems done in a style reminiscent of Rossetti (both Dante Gabriel and Christina were much in vogue at the time), and then one of short stories, the best of the group being a long tale of a countess (a salamander spirit) who wanted a soul.[5] The stories are rich in folk and fairy tale elements and have about them a vital moral dimension of good amply rewarded. These two volumes (1896, 1900) appeared in the decade when publishers like David Nutt of Fleet Street sought to meet the public's demand for belles-lettres in inexpensive

---

[4] Twenty years later she urged Houghton Mifflin to re-issue the work in a cheaper edition citing a continuing demand for the book and the probability of good sales spurred by the expiration of Wagner's *Parsifal* copyright. The original plates held by the David Nutt Company were destroyed in a fire, and Mrs Nutt did not wish to bear the expense of a costly reissue. Weston described this project as dear to her heart, especially as she feared the appearance of an inferior translation of Wolfram's poem, and said she would take back her rights to the book, though it would cost her Mrs Nutt's friendship, if Nutt refused to negotiate a reissue. (Letter, March 30, 1914). Nothing came of it.

[5] "I only write such tales when the themes occur to me spontaneously, and the idea is sometimes in my head for years before I work it out." (Letter, March 19, 1919). The tales were "The Ruined Temple" and "Débout, Les Morts!" which had appeared earlier in *The Quest*. Five other tales, now lost, were "Our Lady of Douglas," based on a real experience; "The Ring of Buondelmonte," a historical tale; "The Wolf-Maiden" and "The Convent," tales of pure invention; and "The Leader of Souls." Mrs Nutt would not publish for lack of a market. Houghton Mifflin declined for the same reason. The war was just over and the public had lost its taste for legends and tales of the supernatural.

nicely-bound editions. Weston's was not exactly a new voice, but these minor imaginative works were a further revelation of the many talents of the translator-scholar and purveyor of Germanic mythology. Her stories in the 1900 collection are certainly better than the two tales that have survived among a group she wrote later (probably after 1910), of a "mystical-fanciful character, for which she could not find a publisher in England or America. There followed the Lancelot and Perceval studies; and as she prepared these, she also undertook for David Nutt's Grimm Library the prose translations of Arthurian Romances Unrepresented in Malory, eight slim volumes of then little known but important minor poems (and some major ones like Gottfried's *Tristan*) and accepted a commission from the Encyclopaedia Britannica for twelve articles with bibliographies for their new edition, the eleventh. Her career as a medievalist had begun in 1894; by the turn of the century she was fully launched as a leading translator and interpreter of medieval texts; by 1910 she was the foremost English Arthurian and folklorist, a title she was to keep until her death.

Her views on Grail origins were by now running counter to the conventional wisdom, and as she leaned more and more to Welsh rather than Irish provenance of Grail tradition, the strains among the Celticists grew. *The Quest of the Holy Grail* in 1913 set forth fairly and fully the three leading theories of Grail origins, Christian, Celtic, Ritual, which she favored. Also, between 1910 and 1913 she compiled two textbooks for Houghton Mifflin as part of the Chief English Poets series. W. H. Schofield of Harvard, with whom she corresponded, had suggested such a project in 1905 and later introduced her to the American publisher who would issue the work in two parts, considerably more than the original plan – *Romance, Vision and Satire* in 1912, containing alliterative poems, and two years later *Chief Medieval English Poets*. A minor but very unpleasant falling-out between the two followed publication. Schofield complained to her that he had received too little credit for his share in her work, but Weston brushed aside his claims as overrating the value of his initial suggestions. Many of the works she translated for this series had never before appeared in modern English. She resented the reader's suggestion that she revise the rhyme form and reminded the Houghton Mifflin editor of her established reputation as a translator (so she thought of herself in these years). She claimed to have consulted Kerr and Raleigh on the appropriate verse form and chided the publisher for relying on the reviewer's judgement instead of his own good taste! Needless to say, there were no revisions. To her public she declared herself to be the best beneficiary of her labours for having become acquainted with non-Arthurian medieval literature.

She hoped to come to the United States for a lecture tour of women's colleges and clubs in order to promote her book. She had a considerable following in America and was an experienced lecturer with appearances before the London Lyceum and Folk-Lore Society to her credit. In fact, she had just recently returned from Paris to accept a speaking engagement at Newnham College, the women's college of Cambridge.[6] When Houghton Mifflin declined to arrange a college series, she dropped her plans. So long and expensive a journey should have professional use. She may well have visited the United States at another time (she spoke of her American friends as members of the leading women's clubs in New York and Washington as well as among university faculties), but for now seemed content to begin work on a new book while shuttling back and forth from Paris for holidays with her sister and niece in Carshalton, a small town not far from London. She was in Bayreuth when the war broke out, and in the great haste to get back to England, an unprecedented two-week ordeal, lost all her luggage in Germany. Her possessions remained in Paris, but by late 1914 she was back in her Paris flat. In 1915 she wrote two strong anti-German pamphlets to make the French case better known, particularly to those groups in English universities who had expressed strong pacifist sentiments towards Germany, a position she deplored. During the years of war interest in medieval literature had waned; students of the period were scarce and university courses were disappearing. This collapse after decades of intense interest is reflected even in the long hiatus in her own career. Her sojourns in England lengthened, but she managed to return to Paris in the summer of 1916 to resume work on the book that was to contain her "final views" on the subject of Grail origins. That book was to be *From Ritual to Romance*. In 1919 Cambridge University Press accepted the manuscript for publication the following year.

War in Logres

There were from the first two schools of Arthurian romance. The Insular or Celtic held that the tradition began in Celtic myth and folklore and was transmitted by Welsh bards to the Breton conteurs. This was Weston's view. Then there were the Continentals or Inventionists, who admitted no Welsh (Celtic) Arthurian tradition. The legends had formed in Armorica, came to the attention of Chrétien de Troyes, who was the first to make use of them. Before Chrétien, the abyss. Much of the controversy hinged on

---

[6] Jane Harrison, Newnham's distinguished Hellenist, had left Cambridge by then to take up life in Paris.

dating. One date more or less accurate makes little difference to most readers outside the academy; certainly the dispute over a forty-year range in which an 800-year-old poem may have been composed is not the stuff to set modern pulses racing. But to earlier scholars who struggled to establish texts and lines of derivation, describing the evolution of romance depended on a reliable chronology. Out of the complex tangle of romance, each school attempted approximate dating, less from an intrinsic interest in texts, than as a way of buttressing theories about the evolving Arthurian tradition. To complicate matters, each side had a rather narrow time line to fix, as most acknowledged that the several romance cycles had been composed by the 1230s.

In an early major work, *The Legend of Sir Perceval*, Weston set out to examine all romances of the Perceval cycle, a formidable undertaking considering that with few exceptions the manuscripts were held by different libraries across Europe. She brushed off the task merely as "not impossible" despite the magnitude; after all, she was not presenting critical editions, only grouping texts for purposes of comparison. She concentrated on the First and Second Continuations of Chrétien's *Conte del Graal*, the so-called Pseudo-Wauchier and Wauchier Continuations, for she was convinced that within these works was contained a body of Arthurian tradition that had flourished well before Chrétien's time and proclaimed confidently that as a result of facts uncovered in her study long-held views would have to be revised.[7] She held that the *Perceval* of Chrétien de Troyes was composed from a very old tale existing in variants even before Chrétien wrote, that extant versions of the *Perceval* contained fragments of Chrétien's source, and that by examining all versions, a coherent reconstruction of the original tale could be developed. She rejected outright that the book of Philip of Flanders mentioned by Chrétien as his source was available to Chrétien alone and not to others as well.

When she turned to the manuscript, she found before her Potvin's defective Mons texts, a copy whose many errors obscured the contribution to the Perceval story made by Wauchier. In Wauchier lay the proof of British origins of the tale. The key figure was Gawain, and the solution postulated collections of short lais, which she called "The Geste of Sir Gawain." This *geste* group had been fed by two sets of adventures: the first, of a primitive character, was the Chastel Orguellous group (this

---

7 The *Perceval* studies continued to be consulted for some time for the summaries and discussion of all *Perceval* manuscripts, but she failed to convince the opposition. In her last book, *The Romance of Perlesvaus*, she expressed regret that she had moved so few scholars to research along the lines proposed in *The Legend of Sir Perceval*.

collection, which recounts Gawain's adventures at this castle, Ferdinand Lot had designated the Pseudo-Wauchier Continuation, now called the First Continuation); the Second, a more polished and literary narrative, was the Chastel Merveilleus group (events retold by Wauchier in the Second Continuation). Chrétien had drawn an early Gawain poem into his *Perceval*, but Wauchier, by which she meant the author of the First and Second Continuations (that identification rejected by modern scholars), was composing from the actual *geste* tradition into which the adventures of Perceval had been introduced at some point. In other words, Wauchier's source was earlier than Chrétien's, thus closer to the original tradition.

It was this unshakable theory of lost hypothetical originals that drew heavy fire from her critics, not, as one would suppose, the more flamboyant theory of ritual origins of the Grail. She presented her case first in *The Legend of Sir Gawain* (1897), then in *The Legend of Sir Lancelot* (1901), followed by *The Three Days' Tournament* published separately as an appendix, and completed this major phase of her work with *The Legend of Sir Perceval*, two volumes (1906, 1909). In *Romania*, the Paris-based journal founded by Gaston Paris where many battles were fought out, she refined points and met objections of other critics, these coming largely by way of long reviews of her books.

The Continental school insisted that as there was no extant poem earlier than Chrétien's; the tradition began with him. She and other Celticists had to argue backwards from Chrétien, his continuators, and other romances (some of much later date) that many episodes seemingly derived from Chrétien actually derived from traditional materials anterior to Chrétien. The Continental side had only to point to existing texts, whole or fragmentary. When two similar adventures appeared in different texts, that usually indicated that one writer had borrowed the tale from the other, changing the details as he saw fit, a common practice among medieval writers. Weston maintained that this was not the case, that there existed a common source from which both writers drew independently, and that this source originated in the British Isles.

The eminent American medievalist James Douglas Bruce (a life-long opponent of her views) accused her of believing that the "period of really great Arthurian romance" pre-dated Chrétien. This she had not said (though she believed it in part); her point was that a tradition had lived and flourished and Chrétien's audience was familiar with the main lines of adventures that he borrowed and popularized further. She was certainly unawed by Chrétien's reputation and the esteem in which he was held by her German contemporaries, the group that had long dominated Arthurian studies. Chrétien's "overrated" talents, she said, reposed in graceful language applied to familiar tales adjusted to court conventions.

She found hard to take seriously Chrétien's claim (in *Erec*) that he had written a Tristan poem. And even if he had done so, the world had lost little by its not having survived. She found him incapable of dealing adequately with such a theme as we find in *Tristan*: "the absolutely human truthfulness of that wonderful love story [was] all utterly beyond his grasp."[8] Her deflation of Chrétien was aimed squarely at the German Foerster (Chrétien's editor), Golther, and Hoffmann, to whom Chrétien was not only the great poet-innovator of romance, but the first poet to combine shreds of piecemeal inchoate tales into masterpieces. She went on: there was, moreover, a respectable, flourishing Arthurian tradition before Chrétien – a living one, and Chrétien stood at a *late* point in the evolution, not at the beginning.

An agitated Bruce spoke of the "greatest mischief" being done by over relying on the Continuations and cited Weston specifically, adding a comment on her mistaken belief in the existence of the Welsh bard Bleheris. There were other Celticists certainly, others who held to the Insular theory, but none so provoking as she, if we are to judge from the hundreds of times she is cited by Bruce and the other spokesmen of the Continental school. Bruce was relatively restrained, gentlemanly, despite the burden of his own "Jessie Weston Complex," but the choler of the Germans, particularly Foerster and Golther, was unabating – the more so as Miss Weston seemed undaunted by their criticism. Even those more or less sympathetic to her views, like the Swiss Ernst Brugger, could be severe. Some of the resentment was mean-spirited. She was a woman moving into a man's world; equally distressing, she was English encroaching on German territory: ". . . has not the writer . . . been solemnly warned off ground sacred to scholars of another sex, and dare we say of another nation?" she wrote. Her views would turn to ashes, warned Golther. "She has been told that when Arthurian criticism is further advanced such crude efforts as hers will not be so much as mentioned! She has been accused of "building in the air" without any foundation in fact, while the learned reviewer turned with relief to the solid labors of one who really "dealt with the facts and knew his sources' – the facts in question being the statement that Chrétien's continuators had no sources save his poems, and the authority relied upon, the mendacious Mons!"[9] She, in turn, found the Foerster-Golther school "old-fashioned," "stifling," "fettering" in its refusal to allow that where two texts resembled each other there could be a common source. There were eminent scholars who normally stood outside the fray, W. W. Greg for one,

8 LSP, Vol. I, pp. 230–31.
9 The error-ridden Perceval manuscript edited by Potvin in 1866.

ready to join her in condemning the narrow-mindedness that was "dragging the honoured reputation of German criticism down." To Greg much of the fault of the German group lay in their relying too heavily on Oskar Sommar's Malory studies, a work filled with "inexcusable blunders."[10]

We must interpret the extraordinary attention paid her by her contemporaries as a sign of her influence as scholar and critic. She dominated English Arthurian studies as *the* specialist in romance literature. Abroad were the Germans and Americans, the latter divided as well, with Kittredge and Brown the spokesmen for Celtic origins. Among the French (who usually regarded her work highly), there were Gaston Paris, Lot, Loth, and Edmond Faral, often divided on the issue of Breton, Celtic, or Chrétien priority. Critics wrote carefully detailed reviews. Brugger, whom she regarded as an honest but very severe critic, reviewed Vol. I of her *Perceval* studies (nineteen pages) and Vol. II (an incredible forty pages!) for *Zeitschrift für französische Sprache und Literatur*. In the blistering criticism of Vol. II, he referred to her hypothetical reconstruction of Borron's verse *Perceval* as "idle child's play" (müssige Spielerei) of questionable or imprecise presumptions on the text. She had been warned against the attempt by friends (Ferdinand Lot and Joseph Bédier) but imprudently went ahead anyway.[11] In journals these battles warmed to a zeal. Weston frequently emphasised an important point by coolly calling upon her opponents to give but an impartial hearing to her theories and so be convinced of their correctness. She claimed always (even to her last work *The Romance of Perlesvaus*) to have approached Arthurian romance with an open mind and been led to her conclusions by the evidence. She pushed her ideas against the columns of entrenched reactionaries, as she would call them, until meeting a Weston challenge became the predictable side issue of Arthurian criticism.

Bruce recognised her impact on the literature by devoting an entire chapter in his important *The Evolution of Arthurian Romance* to "Miss Weston's Gawain-Complex" (the chapter title implying perhaps inadvertently the *idée fixe* of her work *and* mind). Here again, Bruce's claim was that she could produce no convincing evidence that the so-called *Chastel* group ('The Geste of Sir Gawain") ever existed, much less that the continuators of Chrétien's *Conte del Graal* had these tales before them as

[10] Review of *The Legend of Sir Lancelot* in *Folk-Lore*, 12 (1901), 495.
[11] I am grateful to Professor William Roach for calling my attention to this point and to the fact that "for many years Miss Weston was the only scholar who examined *all* the extant MSS of Chrétien's *Perceval* and its Continuations and gave useful descriptions of their contents . . . as early as 1906, long before Hilka (1932) and Micha (1939)."

they wrote. If another romance did exist, Bruce allowed, it must have been a contemporary one, a formal poem like Chrétien's "and not an episodic poem . . . such as Miss Weston supposes, that had lived in oral tradition for centuries."[12] Her belief that popular tradition had fed many of the adventures was brushed aside as inventions of her own folkloristic fancy. Where even Bruce could not ignore the folklore elements in *Perceval*, he attributed these to Chrétien, adding that Chrétien was the first poet to combine old folk motifs in a literary poem. Weston had dated the existence of a Gawain legend from the tenth century, but had no proof to show. For Bruce and the others, Gawain was born in Geoffrey of Monmouth's comment that Gawain was a valiant nephew of Arthur. From Geoffrey to Wace, thence to Chrétien: "We have no early short episodic poems about Gawain and no evidence that there were any."

It was clear that neither side would convince the other in the matter of the Gawain lais, or the use by Chrétien's continuators of a source earlier than Chrétien.[13] The first volume of *Perceval* studies, though controversial in the matter of the Holy Blood legend of Fécamp and the ritual theory, was welcomed for its summaries of all extant manuscripts of Chrétien's *Perceval* and Continuations. The second volume included a printing of the Modena MS. of the Didot-*Perceval*.[14] Potvin years before had published the Didot-*Perceval*, a prose rendering of a lost poem by

---

[12] *The Evolution of Arthurian Romance*, II (Baltimore, 1923), p. 94.
[13] In 1925 she was satisfied that Lot and Bruce had been proved wrong in rejecting her theories. In "The Apple Tree Mystery in Arthurian Romance" she presented "what is manifestly the original" of an incident in both the Didot-*Perceval* and Wauchier's continuation, "proving up to the hilt" her contention of "mutual interdependence and dependence upon a common source." In 1929 Ernst Brugger, also at work on the Apple Tree incident, reached similar conclusions from different evidence.
[14] An edition of *The Didot-Perceval According to the Manuscripts of Modena and Paris*, ed. William Roach (Philadelphia, 1941), is the standard work on the subject. Weston's text of Modena contained many errors and misreadings, leading William Roach to question whether she had intended originally to print the transcript made several years earlier (see Roach, pp. 4–9). Weston remarked that a copy of Modena had been prepared for Gaston Paris by Giulio Camus but could not now be found. She may have printed her transcription to fill the void created by the loss of G. Paris' copy. She assumed scholars would adopt her suggestion that the Didot-*Perceval* now be called the *Prose Perceval*, and Lot and Pauphilet did so. However, most preferred the original title for the sensible reason that the work was everywhere known as the Didot-*Perceval*, and calling it something else would cause confusion. She dropped the new title from her later works but referred to the Modena-*Perceval* or Didot-Modena *Perceval*, as did Mary Williams later.

Robert de Borron, the author of the *Joseph* and *Merlin* that had given a decidedly Christian colouring to the origins of the Grail. As the Didot manuscript was defective, scholars welcomed access to a printed superior text. But the controversy soon erupted, again over lost originals. To early Arthurian scholars the question of whether Borron had ever written a poem concerning Perceval of which this, the prose version, was the only record was hotly argued. Weston, G. Paris, and Brugger, without necessarily agreeing on all points, argued from internal indications that yes, this was a prose rendering of Borron's lost conclusion of the Joseph-Merlin romances. Others claimed that the Didot-*Perceval* was derived not from Borron but from Chrétien and Wauchier's Continuation, that there had never been a Borron *Perceval*, and all further speculation was useless. They were irritated by Weston's insistence in *The Legend of Sir Perceval* and in articles that such a poem existed, proved by her own reconstruction printed in the second volume. She was accused by Bruce of "invincible prejudice against acknowledging that any extant work could be used by the author of any other extant work," and of attempting to change the plan and tone of Borron's work. Out of this came yet another round of rebuttals. But it was clear that dating again was at the root of the problem, for if Weston was right about the prose *Perceval* then the Arthurian prose cycles (Vulgate romances and the pseudo-Robert de Borron cycle) had developed out of this work and Perceval not Galahad was the original hero of the Grail quest, as she had maintained from the beginning. She said that once Galahad was established as the Grail winner (as in the Vulgate), no writer of romance would resuscitate Perceval in that role; thus, the Didot-*Perceval* must be of much earlier date than the great cyclic *Queste*. Furthermore, the prose *Perlesvaus*, which Bruce and Lot had dated very late, must be the earliest form of the quest after the original work (that is, the first stage of evolution). As Weston grew older, she became intractable on this point. She eagerly awaited William Nitze's critical edition of the *Perlesvaus* to provide conclusive proof. Meanwhile, convinced that in the *Perlesvaus* lay the means to refute her critics once and for all, she embarked on a full study of that romance, first in journals, then in book form.

The Celtic Branch

There were fundamental differences separating the Celtic, or Insular, group from the Continental, or Inventionist. Their studies proceeded from opposing basic assumptions. Each could demonstrate the truth of its view more or less to the satisfaction of its *confrères* and the chagrin of the opposite member. Yet within the Celtic group there was seldom perfect accord.[15] The eminent Celticists were Nutt, Rhys, Brown, and Kittredge, with Loomis soon to join the company. With Alfred Nutt's death in 1910, Weston, in direct line of descent in Grail theories, though not a confirmed Celticist and never to be one, assumed the leadership among the folklorists. She had little knowledge of Celtic languages and was very cautious in the matter of roots and derivations of names, always consulting first with the Welsh or Irish linguist before discussing etymologies in print. Obviously more comfortable with comparisons of texts, she doubted that reliable proofs could be derived from roots. "Names are such tricky things," she wrote to John Evans in 1921 – "I have been so thoroughly scared off this ground by Brugger's wild flights of derivatives."[16] The cautious critic, reviewing Loomis's first book *Celtic Myth and Arthurian Romance*, expressed her doubts about derivations so: "I do not propose to touch upon it here, preferring to leave a discussion of the many problems raised to those better versed in these bewildering transmutations, the outcome of which appears to me to be in the present case, as in that of Rhys's work, the creation of a mythic protoplastic mass, in which all individuality is lost, and any section of which equals any other section." She rejected Loomis's derivation of Gurgalain in favour of Kittredge's, and considered his derivation of Lancelot's name from Welsh originals "clearly impossible and unnecessary . . . Lancelot is not a Celtic name."

Roger S. Loomis had been an enthusiastic partisan of her claims for the existence of the Welsh Bleheris as the conteur of the main body of

---

15 Loomis preferred the name Traditionalists for this group because of the traditional folklore elements of Arthurian romance.

16 In a review of *The Legend of Sir Perceval*, II, W. P. Ker (whom Weston thought the greatest living medievalist) reminded her that in undertaking the reconstruction of the original verse from Borron's *Perceval* "nothing less than the perfection of philology is required" if the work is to stand criticism. Her competence in modern and medieval languages was widely acknowledged, but her attempts at recreating verse forms from prose fell far short of the mark. Perhaps she remembered the success of the 1894 *Parzival* translations: two misreadings from the German in 2400 lines, she claimed.

Arthurian tradition – the same Bleheris (or Bleri, or Bledhericus) cited by Geraldus Cambrensis, Chrétien, and Wauchier as a real person, and by two of these writers as a famous storyteller.[17] Loomis, a new entrant into these disputes, suggested further that the poet was a transmitter in French rather than Welsh (she had been equivocal about the language, but later wrote of Bleheris as a French-speaking Welshman). Loomis added that Bleheris' *contes* were already altered by contact with continental forces. In other matters, he endorsed her claims for an early date of the *Elucidation*, a prologue of sorts attached to the Mons *Perceval*, which Bruce insisted had derived from Chrétien and the Continuations.[18] Most important was his enthusiastic support of Weston's work in the ritual theory. He praised *From Ritual to Romance* as a worthy book full of her "characteristic flashes of insight," and defended her theory of initiation against critics who questioned the reliability of her evidence. He cited the endorsement of authorities on ritual and cultural anthropology: Sidney Hartland's "scholarly, scientific work through and through," Jane Harrison's "conviction of its rightness," Francis Cornford's "self-evident [argument]," et al. With these appraisals Loomis concurred fully, reserving only a different view on transmission and later development of the material. In his Chapter XXVI, he accepted Weston's position as given in *From Ritual to Romance*.[19]

This warm support was not to last long. By 1930, two years after her death, he had retreated from positions stated in *Celtic Myth*, but reaffirmed his basic concurrence with her theory of Grail origins in fertility rites and the sexual nature of the Grail King's wounds. However, he no longer believed the ritual was sexual in nature, nor that the Lance and Grail were sexual symbols originating in ancient Mystery religions.[20]

Their interests had never been identical; there was considerable latitude within the Insular school for adherents to strike out independently on a different tack while still adhering to the Celtic origins position though

---

[17] This *conteur* pre-dated Chrétien de Troyes and was claimed to be Wauchier's source.

[18] The persistent seeking of lost originals struck Bruce and others as sheer obstinacy: "As she does virtually always in such instances," he complained, speaking of her claim that the *Elucidation* and Wauchier's continuation derived from a common source. Where Bruce must concede the point, he did so unhappily, as in, "She is probably right, but one cannot decide positively," *Evolution*, II, p. 87. The Inventionists were not beyond a little invention of their own, as in Bruce, II, p. 127.

[19] Loomis's panegyric of quotations is taken from Weston's article on the death of Bruce in the *Bulletin of the Board of Celtic Studies*, 2 (1924), 176.

[20] *Revue Celtique*, 47 (1930), 39–62.

Weston was now obviously promoting the Attic not Celtic origins of the Grail. When Loomis asked her to review *Celtic Myth and Arthurian Romance*, she agreed but did not welcome the task. His book had been highly complimentary ("most amiable to me," she wrote Mary Williams), but if flattered by his rich praise, she did not let it interfere with her judgement. She told Mary Williams that Loomis suffered from a "Curoi Complex" – using here modern psychological parlance – "sees Curoi everywhere . . . He seems to have started on the theory that as *some* of the Arthurian heroes may be traced back to Irish origins, all must be, and he forces the names into a framework in the most arbitrary manner."[21] The work was confused, repetitious. Some of his conclusions she found absurd, for instance, that Gawain-Lancelot-Perceval derived from the same character, or that "themes of world-wide diffusion are all related to Curoi." But the fatal defect, she said, was his ignoring literary transmission: "By the end of the thirteenth century the mythic had become the folk-lore tradition. The stories had been told and retold till their original significance had been forgotten." The Grail ritual could never have been derived from the "coarsely pagan ritual" proposed by Loomis.[22]

Her review was harsh: Loomis's method was "radically unsound," he ignored literary progression and gradual growth, he supposed writers of romance to be fully aware of the character of their material, his use of texts was fundamentally uncritical. Further, she challenged his interpretation of the Modena archivolt, his "elaborate assumptions" of *Gareth and Lynette*; his case, she said, was built of dogmatic assertions "but with a regrettable lack of critical argument." She flatly rejected identifying Perceval's sister with the Grail Messenger as a jumble of confused misconceptions and sheer misstatement. Even where she naturally agreed with his theory of Grail origins in vegetation rites, Loomis's proposed reconstruction of Irish Grail ritual was dismissed as impossible of generating the Grail romances. On the other hand, she met his objection to her interpretation of the Grail Mysteries as mystical though he had merely referred in a footnote to the lack of textual evidence. Finally, she called upon him to find even a trace of Arthur in Irish romance, while in Wales Arthur was still a living tradition. "Is not this silence sufficient refutation of his extravagant claims?"[23] All in all, a bruising rebuke that Loomis did not immediately answer in print as he did similar criticism by French critic Ferdinand Lot.

Later, in books and articles, he responded. Where Weston had traced

21 Letter, May 29, 1927.
22 Letter, June 3, 1927.
23 *Modern Language Review*, 32 (1928), 243–48.

Celtic sources of medieval literature there was praise.[24] He regarded her first book, *The Legend of Sir Gawain*, the soundest because she had found parallels in a Gawain adventure in two German romances and a Cuchulainn tale, and had noted resemblances in Gawain's Chastel Merveilleus episode and "The Voyage of Bran."[25] (This, incidentally, was the book Weston was least pleased with because she thought she had arrived at her views too hastily.) In an article on Gawain he noted briefly that she had abandoned the "promising start she had made of the study of Celtic origins."[26] He claimed "error and ignorance" in accepting thirty years before the Priest of Nemi view and acknowledged the correctness of Lot and Brugger in having rejected his *Celtic Myth* on those grounds, but reasserted his correctness in all other matters set forth. Once again, in 1948, he resurrected in order to renounce his past adherence to Weston's theory, this time discarding the last tie: the testing of Perceval derived from a fertility rite.[27] And in 1963 in *The Grail from Celtic Myth to Christian Symbol*, he repeated his retraction of adherence to "Dr Jessie Weston's ingenious hypothesis concerning the Grail and Lance for lack of valid and clearly pertinent evidence."[28]

Jessie Weston knew as well as any one else that few ideas outlast one's own time, and in the world of Arthurian scholarship there could be friendships, courtesy, and mutual respect where there was also profound disagreement. Sometimes the strains showed; writers became testy crusaders for a point of view, and the reputedly gentler temper of the scholar flared as another round went off. The debate was all the livelier for the heat. Loomis owed much of the early development of his thought to her work, and benefitted from her friendship and encouragement despite reasonable differences of opinion. He acknowledged the part Weston played in his career, implicitly in the retractions, and directly in a passage in *Arthurian Tradition and Chrétien de Troyes*: ". . . here I shall limit myself to naming those who have made the largest and most significant contribution to the right understanding of the *Matière de Bretagne*: Gaston Paris, Bédier, Zimmer, Brugger, Nutt, Jessie Weston, and Gertrude Schoepperle. All these attacked fundamental and formidable questions, and though they sometimes attacked each other and were, being human, fallible, they advanced the limits of our knowledge in a large way and into obscure regions" (p. 6).

[24] *Romance Philology*, 9 (1956), 163.
[25] *Romania*, 79 (1958), 50.
[26] *Journal of English and Germanic Philology*, 42 (1942), 153.
[27] *Arthurian Tradition and Chrétien de Troyes* (New York, 1948), p. lx.
[28] *The Grail* (New York and Cardiff, 1963), pp. ix–x.

The reader is left to speculate whether the force of that strong personality or the sheer persistence of a theory widely rejected by the academy "for lack of valid and clearly pertinent evidence" has kept Weston's ghost in touch with modern audiences.

The Study of Folklore

Serious interest in folklore began early in the nineteenth century in Germany with the publication of Grimm's *Kinder und Hausmärchen* and *Deutsche Mythologie*. Rooted in romantic nationalism, the study of folklore actually had its beginnings in philological analysis and speculation. Mainly as a consequence of the work of Oxford Sanskrit scholar Max Müller, much of the century was dominated by the philological school until overthrown by the challenges of Müller's fellow Oxonian Andrew Lang and by Sidney Hartland. These "folklorists" came against the philologists with a full battery of arguments and methods developed by the rising new science of comparative anthropology. Müller was a brilliant "Aryanist," who had begun his career as a classicist; as a young man he became infatuated with Indic culture, and from the 1860s to his death in 1900 insisted in lectures, books, and journals that Indo-European myths derived ultimately from divine genealogies in the Vedic hymns.[29] In a remote time when the Aryans spoke a common tongue, the names and epithets of the gods were known to all but after the great migrations began, meanings of the names were corrupted through natural processes and myths grew up as a "diseased language" to explain forgotten etymologies. The philologists held that in the Sanskrit hymns of the Rig-Veda were preserved the names of these deities, and all Greek, Norse, Celtic myths – all myths of Indo-Aryan origination – were traceable to solar gods of the Vedas, specifically in the roots of words.

To folklorists the most objectionable aspect of the solar myth theory (as it was called) was the presumption that the everyday speech of the ordinary pre-historic Aryan was at the poetic level of the Vedas; that analysis of roots and metaphors could reveal original meanings of the gods' names; that the intellectual level of Indo-European stock was considerably advanced over that of their descendants, so much so that the race had declined rather than advanced with the passage of time (evolution

[29] Aryan is interchangeable with Indo-European. Obviously the word carried none of its modern connotations.

theory insisted on progress over the ages, not decline) – all as a result of corrupt etymologies. Müller's hypothesis necessarily meant that the original Aryans were possessed of a far more refined state of religious feeling than his opponents were willing to concede. Lang and Hartland (among others) were quick to point out, as folklorist Wilhelm Mannhardt had earlier, that where it was essential that philologists agree on Sanskrit-Greek equivalents, there was often disagreement (sometimes two or three widely different solar gods were derived from the same Sanskrit name). Of course some striking parallels certainly existed, like the Dyaus-Zeus example, and no one would dispute the philological blundering of folk etymologies, but Müller and his followers had gone too far. The position of the philologists was further eroded by their refusal to admit non-Aryan (thus not philologically comparable) peoples into their solar theory although similar myths among other groups clearly existed, either having developed independently or by diffusion. Once the solar myth school had placed origins in the Vedas, to admit like myths in other groups to which the Vedas were unknown was undermining to their theory. The philological school had its hey-day as part of the general ascendancy of German scholarship in England, but died of its own excesses in attempting to meet the challenge of anthropology. With the death of Müller, its foremost champion, in 1900, the philological school of comparative mythology quickly faded, leaving behind a strengthened group of folklorists busily engaged in a systematic study of customs and belief.[30]

To comparative folklorists, by no means of one mind in all matters, the folktale contained the surviving vestiges of savage practice and tradition. The tales had been transmitted orally and adapted to conditions existing in their new home, but given what Lang insisted was the "oneness of human nature" parallel tales could develop independently in different cultures. So, tales, even the sequence of episode, could originate in the common beliefs of different peoples passing through similar evolutionary stages. These stages – from savage to barbarous to civilized – could be studied in "their living representatives among various existing races" (Mannhardt) that only now had attained an intellectual evolution resembling that which cultivated people had passed through long before. Natural selection working through social progress had left the peasant behind but preserved in his traditional stories and beliefs the older ways though their meanings were by now forgotten. Myths and traditions

---

[30] A detailed account of the debate and consequences is given by Richard Dorson in "The Eclipse of Solar Mythology," *Journal of American Folklore*, 68 (1955), 393–416.

passed on in tales and customs would shed light on the whole history of the irrational elements in mythology and religion.[31]

An intensely curious British public could follow the philologist-anthropologist debate while at the same time savoring the heavy doses of folklore of all nations issuing from the nation's presses in a steady stream of books and articles. It was soon clear, given the mass of folklore material being gathered by missionaries, explorers, and ethnologists, that truth was on the side of the folklorist. In 1878 the Folk-Lore Society was founded; its journal *Folk-Lore* became a powerful voice of the newly arrived science, a step-sister of anthropology.[32] There lacked only a Frazer to complete the ascendency.

Such is the fame of Sir James Frazer's *The Golden Bough* that the many makers and shapers of the anthropological school (whom Frazer repeatedly acknowledged) have been overshadowed and forgotten (for instance, foremost spokesman Andrew Lang is largely remembered today for his fairy tale collections). With publication in 1890 of this highly literate study of ritual magic, comparative folklore and anthropology leaped to a new dimension. The public was eager for a sustained application of the inductive method to folklore and traditional beliefs no matter how damaging this might prove to its own favourite faiths and shibboleths. However fondly we hold to notions of Victorian priggishness, the truth is that by the end of the century dogmatism and orthodoxy were in retreat, and the public was more open-minded and tolerant of ideas than it had ever been before or would be in the era that followed. The implications of a universe mechanised out of human comprehension had not yet unsettled the confidence of these sturdy Victorians, pleased with their intellectual achievements and practical in all matters secular and religious. Frazer, standing philosophically with the Positivists between Darwinian natural selection and Freud's darker visions of psychological necessity as powerful as the biological (though Frazer refused to read Freud), was an undogmatic researcher of human behavior applying the inductive method to the past for the immediate profit of the present generation. The systematic study of custom and belief was after all the inevitable continuation of the nineteenth-century conviction that man is the measure of all things.[33] Utilitarianism, the rise of biological sciences,

---

[31] See the Preface to the First Edition of *The Golden Bough* (London, 1890), pp. xi–xii.

[32] *Folk-Lore* was the title adopted in 1890. The journal was called *Folk-Lore Record* to 1882, then *Folk-Lore Journal* to 1890.

[33] *The Golden Bough*, Third Edition (London, 1911), 27. The study of folklore had moral utility as well. Sidney Hartland insisted that this knowledge was

the study of history as evolutionary process rather than as rise and fall of civilisations, the new criticism in Bible study that ignored the metaphysical in favour of historical-archeological truth, above all Darwinism and its insistence on inescapable biological forces acting through all living things – these converged to produce the precept that myth and religion had also evolved from a lower to a higher form. Certainly, the irrational side of religion had been eradicated among the higher races in keeping with the laws of natural selection (Victorian religion was the proof of it), but magic and superstition – the irrational element – were still vital to the practice of religion among savage people.[34]

The Golden Bough is about magic and the sacred kingship, the taboos surrounding the sacred king, and the myth and ritual of the Dying God. Frazer describes the rise of the priest over the magician, that is, religion's ascendancy over magic. So cultures move historically from primitiveness to savagery to civilisation, this last period marked by science, or the accumulation of knowledge. The safety of the priest-king is of prime importance because his life is bound up with natural forces on which the society is dependent. The health of the land depends on his health; his decline can bring the land to ruin. To kill the king before he has lost his sexual powers and replace him with a young, vigourous successor is to insure that the "divine spirit which he has inherited from his predecessors may be transmitted in turn by him to his successor while it is still in full vigour and has not yet been impaired by the weakness of disease and old

necessary to understand the people one governed: "Effectively to teach a savage people higher morality, to impose upon barbarians the laws of a higher civilisation, you must first penetrate the modes of thought, you must learn how they regard themselves and the external world." This is best done through the study of the products of such people, that is, their folklore. *Mythology and Folktales*, 7 (London, 1900), pp. 14–15.

34 By *savage* is meant a special mental condition described several times by Lang as holding to belief in magic and sorcery, in the existence of souls of the dead and their ability to inhabit bodies of birds and animals or dwell in a spiritual world, in the life and generative powers of all created things, in the spirit or strength located in a part of the body (as in hair or liver). The savage holds natural objects to be intelligent and that men may be metamorphized into planets or stars and that solar phenomena are persons. He believes in the spirits of woods and water, the power of animals to protect him, and his descent from natural objects (totemism). See Andrew Lang, *Myth, Ritual and Religion*, I (London, 1906), pp. 34, 48–62. Holding a totally different view of ancient peoples, Max Müller had maintained mankind's high intellectual ability from the beginning of the mythopoeic age demonstrable in mastery of language, in Oxford Essays, *Comparative Mythology*, ed. A. Smythe Palmer (London, 1909; reprinted New York, 1977).

age."[35] Frazer's studies of the Dying and Resurrected God led him to the conclusion that primitive deities were vegetation spirits (as first proposed by Mannhardt), and that seasonal rituals were sacred dramas enacted in imitation of the cyclic rise and fall of all living creatures.[36]

Frazer's contribution in 300 books, articles, and other pieces to practically every department of humanistic study has been recognised, but none of his other works had so profound an effect on how we understand primitive religious practices as *The Golden Bough*. The book touched countless writers and readers of his and our generation either directly or through criticism, reference, outright borrowing or symbolism in art.[37] He stands with Darwin and Freud as early shapers of modern man's view of himself in relation to his traditions and deeper religious impulses echoed in renewable myths. Nevertheless, many of his views could not stand up against the challenge of better evidence. He has been criticised for his poetic, digressive style, for uncritically accepting the word of missionaries and travellers to distant places while he worked in the comfort of his home, for not knowing the languages of the people he interpreted in his books.[38] His methods were found wanting, and his approach suffered from an evolutionist bias that warped every conclusion. Major objections arise from vastly improved research techniques developed in the age following Frazer's, and they are doubtless justified. Even Frazer expected his conclusions to be overthrown when new information came to light. That open-minded seeking after truth utilising the best methods available characterised the man and his work. That nothing was permanent (including his solutions) had been a lesson driven into the intellectual by the powerful rationalist hammer. Frazer called dogmatism the enemy of

[35] *The Golden Bough*, IV, p. 27.
[36] Frazer's original two-volume edition of 1890 was expanded to three in 1900. By 1915 a third edition of twelve volumes plus supplementary volume had appeared. Frazer issued a one-volume abridgement in 1922.
[37] John Vickery in *The Literary Impact of the Golden Bough* (Princeton, 1973) finds a connection between the late Victorian artistic imagination and the impulses behind Frazer's narrative style. He gives a suggestive account of complex forces, utilitarian, esthetic, and spiritual, affecting Frazer and his contemporaries (pp. 28–37). The effects are reciprocal, with Frazer's account of dying gods and divine kings fed by "the Victorian imagination obsessed with the concrete." Vickery quotes the opening of Tennyson's "Deum," a "Frazerian juxtaposition of ancient Mediterranean worship and contemporary savagery." Tennyson was read to from Frazer's work as he sat for his portrait in 1891.
[38] See Theodore Gaster's summary of criticism in *The New Golden Bough* (New York, 1959), pp. xv–xx and *passim*.

science, admitted his solutions were provisional, and invited correction. The overriding goal was truth, and the method by which truth was to be sought was comparative. Nothing speaks so directly of his purpose as this statement: "The instrument for the detection of savagery under civilisation is the comparative method, which, applied to the human mind, enables us to trace man's intellectual and moral evolution just as, applied to the human body, it enables us to trace his physical evolution from lower forms of animal life. There is, in short, a Comparative Anatomy of the mind as well as of the body, and it promises to be no less fruitful of far reaching consequences, not merely speculative but practical, for the future of humanity."[39]

Frazer clearly separated the great moral monuments of a people from their more brutal beginnings and looked forward with modified English progressivism to a "nobler humanity of the future" for all mankind. In this sentiment of his later years we find tempered the optimism of his predecessors, an optimism impossible to hold to after the modern savagery of World War I pointed up our closer kinship to our primitive ancestors than any enlightened Englishman would have admitted at the turn of the century. Frazer regarded his work as continuing the pioneer ideas first proposed by classicist William Robertson Smith, his teacher at Trinity College, and carried on by the Cambridge tradition of comparative religion. The past that had for so long been hidden for lack of method was now being pried open by the humanistic science of comparative religion and the study of folklore. *The Golden Bough* directly affected the Cambridge classicists (described further on in this study); it also created more interest in folklore, a circular result, since the study of folklore had been the original stimulus of Frazer's work.

Besides creating an unprecedented interest in the history of religion, folklore led to theorizing about the backgrounds of literature. The collecting of folktales and songs, at first an impulse of Romantic *sehnsucht*, after the 1870s took on urgency: man and his institutions were ephemeral things, all was subject to evolutionary forces – people, ideas, and national antiquities alike. The gathering of tales from the Scottish Highlands in the 1860s and later from Ireland and Wales would save them from extinction, which would have occurred as speakers of the native tongues died out, and also provide folklorists with new stocks of tales for comparison. Celtic literature, however, remained neglected by English universities. Matthew Arnold had called for the systematic study of Celtic literature as early as 1867 in *On the Study of Celtic Literature*, but it was not until the

---

[39] *Folk-Lore in the Old Testament*, Abridged Edition (London, 1923), pp. ix–x.

late 1870s that a chair in Celtic Studies was established at Oxford. This went to Sir John Rhys, eminent Welsh scholar and folklorist. In France the literary folklorists led by Gaston Paris, Emmanuel Cosquin, and Gidéon Huet were already examining Celtic myths for sources of medieval romance, but the interest of British folklorists in this line of research was slow to develop. After 1878 folklore study in England made considerable advances under the sponsorship of the Folk-Lore Society.

Gaston Paris, friend and teacher of many young scholars, founder of *Romania* (an organ for the Celtic point of view), was influential in setting the pace of Grail studies in England, though his views differed in several important respects from the views of those who followed in the line of descent, Nutt and Weston. Weston's Celtic origins theories were shaped by Paris' teaching, then supplemented by contact with Nutt, her close friend and collaborator on the *Parzival* translation. It was Celticist Alfred Nutt who actually set the course for British study of Arthurian romance using comparative methods. His *Studies on the Legend of the Holy Grail* (1888) and the later *Legends of the Holy Grail* (1902) directed readers away from the prominent Continental emphasis on Chrétien de Troyes as sole creator of Arthurian romance and towards Irish sources. Naturally he was opposed by the fiercely loyal Chrétien apologists led by Professors Foerster of Bonn and Golther of Munich, with whom Weston as Nutt's successor was to contend. Grail studies in the nineteenth century were overwhelmingly German and the entry of the English folklorist with theories opposed to the prevailing ones drew fire. German scholars objected philosophically to the evolutionary view "militating as it did against the inventive genius of their idol," as Jessie Weston bluntly charged.[40] She had many professional clashes with the German school, the sharp exchanges increasing after Foerster and Golther's attacks in reviews of Nutt's seminal *Studies in the Legend of the Holy Grail*. Heinrich Zimmer, the noted Indiologist, had criticised Nutt's methods and thus given the cue to the others to follow suit in their own reviews. Nutt was offended by Zimmer's Teutonic irony and what he declared were deliberate misstatements of his position by someone of Zimmer's reputation; stronger criticism was spent on the lesser Foerster and Golther. Nutt replied to his German critics in a long article in French in the *Revue Celtique* (1891), reprinted as an addendum in *Folk-Lore*.

This was the only time he went to print in this manner, determined that

[40] "Alfred Nutt: An Appreciation," *Folk-Lore*, 21 (1910), 513. Sir John Rhys's *Studies in the Arthurian Legend* (1891) brought Welsh analogies of Celtic cauldrons to bear on Grail problems.

his critics should not be approved by default and obviously shaken by an unjustified rebuke of a work esteemed everywhere else.[41]

Alfred Nutt, the foremost folklorist in literature of his day, was typical of the group of exceptional men and women drawn to folklore studies while established in business or government careers. Nutt, born into a publishing family run by his father, did more materially than all others, businessmen or scholars, to popularize folklore studies and provide essential books to the specialist, often at great personal expense. Born in 1856, he was only a child of seven when his father David died, and it was not until he was twenty-two with a strong business education behind him that he took control of the David Nutt Company. After an education at University College, London, and at the Collège de Vitry le François, he went immediately to serve business apprenticeships in Leipzig, Berlin, and Paris. It was during the years spent in Germany that his fascination for Celtic myth was aroused. He returned home to manage the firm until his death in 1910, but what time he had to himself he spent writing or promoting Celtic studies. He founded the Irish Text Society in 1898 and the Honorable Society of Cymmrodorion. He joined the Folk-Lore Society in 1878 and became the publisher of the journal in 1890, the year the journal became *Folk-Lore* and incorporated the *Archaeological Review*. Nutt wrote eleven books, five of them as part of the David Nutt *Popular Studies in Mythology* series, 40–50 page pamphlets on all folklore subjects, several by Jessie Weston. His *Grimm Library* was a more ambitious effort intended for serious students of romance and myth. Weston's studies of Gawain, Lancelot, and Perceval appeared among these issues. These and many other works, most of them not profitable, came from the David Nutt press to serve the cause of educating the public in the serious role folklore played in contemporary religious belief and customs. His devotion to the discipline and its utility is summed up in these closing remarks to the Third International Folk-Lore Congress: "Let me say a final word for the attraction and charm of our study. Call it Anthropology, call it folk-lore, the science of Man in his institutions and beliefs is full of lessons and of enjoyment. We stand on the heights and look backwards on the movement of the Race, we see the wilderness whence it comes, the few straggly paths, that wander, that converge, that are lost in the wold, or in the bush, or meet to become the road, and the beaten highway, and the railway track."

Nutt died in Mélun, France, drowned while attempting to rescue his invalid son who had been thrown into the Seine by his horse. His wife and

---

[41] "Derniers travaux allemands sur la légende du saint Graal," *Folk-Lore*, 2 (1891), i–xlviii.

eldest son carried on the publishing house for a time, even after a serious fire that destroyed equipment and printing plates. But the salad days when folklore flourished under the David Nutt rubric were over. Weston, whom Nutt had published, now sought another publisher in 1913 for *Quest of the Holy Grail*. However, two anti-German pamphlets were issued by the David Nutt Company in 1915. These were books for the moment, indicative of the new directions the company had embarked upon now that the great folklore Celticist was gone.

With Alfred Nutt's death, Weston became the leading figure in Arthurian Grail studies in England.

II

Ritual Theory and From Ritual to Romance

The theory of Celtic origins of Arthurian romance continued to attract adherents. But certain Christian aspects of the Grail legends could not be reconciled with the Celtic theory, mainly how a food-producing talisman of Irish myth could be identified with the most sacred object of Christian ritual. The ritual theory formulated by Weston as a solution in comparative religion answered this difficulty. On the premise that an anthropomorphic god died and then rose in homeopathic representation of nature (Frazer to the letter), the episodes of the Grail legend became intelligible. The comparative method was then used to show the survival of rites resembling those connected with Adonis, Attis, and Tammuz into modern times. The Grail itself is regarded as the vessel of the ritual meal of the ancient vegetation cultus; the celebration carries two meanings: the public one open to all worshippers, and the secret or esoteric meaning open only to the initiated one who has proved himself worthy to enter into the Mysteries – conditions which apply to the heroes of the Grail quest. The quest of the Holy Grail, then, is actually for spiritual revelation, a glimpse of the source of life, and entry into sacred company. Celtic folklore was then searched for remains of the old rituals in the British Isles. By the time Weston came to this solution, romance without ritual was to her mere story.[42]

[42] "We have of recent years learnt to recognise the fact that the beliefs and

This decisive turn in Weston's thinking was the result of the emergence of the ritual school of myth out of the Mystery of the sacred kingship and the Dying and Resurrected God, as described by Sir James Frazer. The opening allegory of *The Golden Bough* – the priest of Nemi at Diana's temple in Aricia – introduces the central act of the Mystery. The slaying of the king of the wood is repeated in vegetation rites in which the corn god dies and is revived, the sacrifice assuring the prospering of the land. As the fertility of the land depended on the health of the priest-king, it was essential that at first sign of diminished vigor the kingship should pass to a successor. To the ritualists, myth is the verbal re-enactment of rite and continues to be spoken long after the memory of the rite has faded.

Frazer's ideas were immediately seized upon by a group of scholars Frazer himself dubbed the Cambridge School of Comparative Religion. Classicists all, they had been deeply affected by nineteenth-century evolutionist euphoria, and were quick to apply ritual theory first to Greek art and literature. The Cambridge School included Jane Harrison of Newnham, F. N. Cornford and A. B. Cook of Frazer's own Trinity; and from Oxford, Gilbert Murray, major spokesman of the group. Frazer himself was not part of the group and gave them little encouragement, preferring always to remain an independent researcher not connected with a particular sect or school of theorists. Actually, the Cambridge School became synonymous with the work of Murray and Harrison through their respective *The Rise of Greek Epic* (1907) and *Themis* (1912) that adopted Frazer's method and hypotheses of ritual penetration of Greek culture. Myths survived in art and literature directly or in symbolic form though the rites from which they came are no longer practised. The ancient rites died out but their memory embodying the deepest truths was preserved.[43]

practices of our remote ancestors enshrined a spirit of extraordinary persistence and vitality; that popular custom and practice today reflect with startling and curious fidelity the popular custom and practice of the past; we know, too, that such continuity of custom and practice is not purely secular, surviving merely in popular celebrations, but may be enshrined in the rites and ceremonies of the Church. Where this is not actually the case, the fact that the special folk practices which are now recognized as nature-cult survivals, coincide frequently, if not invariably, with the ecclesiastical feasts, prove that the Church, where she did not accept and adopt, extended not merely tolerance but patronage." *Quest of the Holy Grail* (London, 1913), p. 100. In *From Ritual to Romance* Weston offers her book as an elucidation of the evolution of religious belief "from Pagan Mystery to Christian Ceremonial" (pp. viii–ix).

43 The ritual theory of origins has lately come under renewed attack for the excesses of its disciples Lord Raglan and Stanley Edgar Hyman. Hyman's

Although she contined to acknowledge the debt of romance to Celtic sources, Weston, a Frazerian folklorist, was the immediate heir of the Murray-Harrison tradition, the first scholar to apply the ritual theories and methods of comparative religion to Grail romance. She was not alone in maintaining the nature origins of the Grail, nor was she the first to do so. Many years before the German Arthurian Karl Simrock had proposed that Arthur was a type of vegetation god destined to return healed of his wounds, and that the Grail represented the "creative power of the slain god" connected to the blood of John the Baptist.[44] As early as 1906, fourteen years prior to publication of *From Ritual to Romance*, Weston raised anew the issue of Grail origins in ancient vegetation rites in a paper read to the Folk-Lore Society and published the following year in *Folk-Lore* as "The Grail and the Rites of Adonis." In 1906 and 1909 she presented the ritual theory of the Grail to a wider audience in the two volumes of *The Legend of Sir Perceval*. Curiously, at the same time, William A. Nitze had worked out a similar theory of ritual origins independently. In "The Fisher King in the Grail Romances," Nitze argued that a vegetation ceremony is at the heart of the Grail procession, and that the Mysteries veiled in the Grail ritual served the double purpose of fructifying nature through a sacrificial feast and initiating the soul into the secret of life.[45] The Holy Grail is an initiation; the Grail as a food-producing vessel is connected with the Eleusinian Mysteries (Weston claimed Asiatic origins), that had been carried to the British Isles and Celtic speakers by Mediterranean people. The Grail legend was the outcome of myths and rites practised by the Celts in Britain and modified by Christian additions.

Clearly, the theories of Weston and Nitze at this time look very much alike with the exception of the Eleusinian or Asiatic point of origin. Nitze

---

indebtedness to Weston is acknowledged in a biographical sketch in *Centennial Review*, IX (1965), 509–21. For a review of modern ritual theory, mostly unsympathetic, see Joseph Fontenrose, *The Ritual Theory of Myth*, Folklore Studies: 18 (Berkeley, 1966). To its critics the danger is that the poetry of *The Golden Bough* far outweighs its science. But Frazer persists despite efforts of modern anthropologists to discredit his work. The best explanation of his continued hold on the discipline and on the imagination is found in B. Malinowski's appreciative account of the Frazer he knew as humanist and teacher and an overview of different approaches in cultural anthropology since Frazer wrote, in "Sir James George Frazer," *A Scientific Theory of Culture* (Chapel Hill, 1944), pp. 179–95.

[44] *Parzival und Titurel* (Stuttgart, 1842); also Ernst Martin's identification of Arthur as Grail King in *Zur Gralsage* (Strassburg, 1880).

[45] *PMLA*, 24 (1909), 365–418.

also stressed the intermediate Celtic stage, which accorded more with the views of Celticists like Nutt, and thought that the Fisher King, not the Grail, was the real problem. The role of the Fisher King, he said, was obscured when medieval romance shifted emphasis from the Fisher King, representative of the life-force, to the quester of the Grail. Of course, both Weston and Nitze insisted on the strength of tradition to carry over rituals from a pre-Christian past and recognised that the mystic conceptions embedded in the legend were close to pre-Christian practice, such as Frazer had described, and what was known of pre-Christian doctrine like the Naasene or Gnostic texts.

Deeper divisions in the Grail-nature ritual terrain developed as Weston argued that the Gawain texts rather than the Perceval held the key to the Grail and that the tradition linking Lance and Grail was established before Chrétien wrote. Nitze said Perceval was the vital figure of the initiation through his matriarchal ties with the Fisher King (rejected by Weston) and that Chrétien had been the first to link Perceval and Grail. They agreed on the three-fold symbolism of the Grail: a vessel of the ritual feast, the source of physical life, the source of spiritual life. But on a crucial point that Lance and Cup were symbols of the generative organs, they differed. He also considered valuable her conclusions on the sexual nature of the Fisher King's wounds, and the syncretism of Attis-Adonis-Osiris cults as they moved westward.

In 1913, Weston restated her belief that only the ritual theory could elucidate the Grail mystery and spoke of the ritualists as an entity distinct from the Celticists. To the ritual theory belonged the discovery of the missing links of a puzzle the Celticists had only partially illuminated. Her position, first insisted upon in "The Grail and the Rites of Adonis," delivered as an address to the Folk-Lore Society in 1906, was fixed in *From Ritual to Romance*, 1920.

William Nitze at that time was a young man from Johns Hopkins, a student of medieval French literature, who was later to lead the Department of Romance Languages at the University of Chicago. His dissertation on the *Perlesvaus* in 1902 and subsequent *PMLA* article on the Fisher King established his reputation and marked the beginning of a longstanding interest in the Old French Grail romance, which was to enrich the field for years to come. Among his students were William Roach and J. Neale Carman. Weston and Nitze corresponded; she referred on several occasions to letters they had exchanged, but none has survived. She often reminded her audience of Nitze's forthcoming edition of *Perlesvaus*, sometimes with impatience at the delay, but did not live to see the work in print. Often mildly critical of each other's solutions to questions of ritual origins and route of transmission, they nevertheless remained on friendly terms. Nitze had decided for the ritual origins theory as a young man;

31

Weston had worked out her views rather late in her career. She held firmly to her belief right to the end, while Nitze later modified his ritual position in favour of one that allowed for Celtic and Byzantine influences on Grail literature, finally abandoning his earlier views in an article on Perceval and the Grail romances in 1949.[46]

When in 1920 *From Ritual to Romance* issued from the Cambridge University Press as a volume in a series of comparative religion and anthropology texts identified with the Cambridge School, Weston reached a wide audience already familiar with Frazer and the special problem of Arthurian romance. Weston had written the book with a general but well-educated audience in mind and conceived of it as a study in comparative religion rather than strictly ritual origins of the Grail of interest to specialists only. That her book was greeted warmly by a literate public still enchanted by Frazer's accounts of the sacred kingship and also by the company of scholars for whom she normally wrote attests to the real durability of the subject, which actually had faded from public notice over the decade of war and upheaval.[47]

For many, Jessie Weston had solved the riddle of the Grail. Enthusiastic readers could argue minor matters like route of diffusion of the ritual, the earliest connection of the Grail with Welsh Perceval tradition, the influence of ecclesiastical symbolism, the fusion of Grail Mysteries and Arthurian tradition, and other points without diminishing her results. Where reviewers were critical, two points in particular stood out. Strangely, there was no bibliography and footnoting was careless.[48] She could easily have forestalled criticism had she attended to her book as scrupulously as she did her notebooks where her sources are credited and

---

[46] Professor William Roach graciously provided this information, originally part of a tribute written for the Year Book of the American Philosophical Society on the occasion of William A. Nitze's death in 1957. An extensive bibliography of Nitze's work appears in *Romance Philology*, 9 (1955), pp. 153–57.

[47] Interest in Grail origins in fertility cults had run its course by 1920 and the subject as a major force in Arthurian studies was considered retired. Weston's book instilled new life into an old question, gathering an even larger public after publication of Eliot's "The Waste Land." "Miss Weston's interpretation of the Grail legend lent itself with peculiar aptness to Mr Eliot's extraordinarily complex mind," said Edmund Wilson in an early appreciation of the book's power to generate poetic images. "The Poetry of Drouth," *The Dial*, 73 (1922), 611–16.

[48] Replying to a complaint that the Old French and German passages should have been translated, she claimed having given in to the pedants who would object to all but the original languages.

which show her extensive reading in ancient myth and ritual, medieval religion and society. She may have thought full annotation unnecessary, even cumbersome, to non-specialists, and risked being called non-scientific by reviewers (which occurred in only a few cases). Or the decision may have been the publisher's considering the larger general audience the book was to reach. Far more serious, however, was the substantive criticism that she had relied too heavily on information supplied by unnamed friends possessing Hermetic or occult knowledge. Those ill-disposed to her theories at the outset pounced on this specious approach to a solution, but even sympathetic critics complained she was on thin ice in drawing conclusions based on evidence impossible to document, therefore unscientific. No mere carping, this defect ultimately unhinged the door she had pried open. Ultimately, but not immediately, for the willingness of an age of rational thinkers, logical positivists, and similar seekers of Truth to accept Weston's solutions while only sometimes critical of her method is indicative of the welcome accorded all ideas, particularly where the writer had an established reputation. This, and the acknowledged fact of the existence of active secret-doctrine societies, which gave a certain legitimacy to the claims of occult knowledge, disarmed real objection to her method at the time.

Why had she used unverifiable sources? The answer was the problem of texts. First, there would be few texts containing secret doctrine committed to books; the point was always that esoteric knowledge was passed among the elect of a group. What texts were available, she made use of. Second, there was only fragmentary evidence that the Mysteries had continued to exist side by side with Christianity into the Middle Ages when they suddenly surfaced in veiled or tangled form in the Grail ceremonies. She wrote: "We are dealing with a matter that antedates our earliest Greek text by a thousand years and is consequently too remote for any direct bearing on the problem of Grail origins." Gnostic books often cited to show the fusion of pagan and Christian elements in an initiation rite in the Mysteries could not be shown to have produced Grail literature a thousand years later. But the anthropological method had proved that ancient practices survived in one form or another in modern customs and beliefs; the researcher gathered data from the living traditions or practitioners of a craft and studied the past through them. Of course, the problem here was verifying the truthfulness of the reports, of being absolutely certain that the informants reporting the continuation of ancient rites into the twentieth century were not merely frauds telling the researcher what she wanted to hear – a charge philologist Max Müller had in fact levelled at the anthropologists when missionaries brought back stories confirming favoured assumptions about savage people. True, she admitted, the evidence could not be traced with the precision of a trade route; the literalist would never be satisfied. She had put before the public her final views on the subject (it was now fourteen years since her address to the Folk-Lore Society). The reception was gratifying.

There was one stinging review in London's influential *The Saturday Review* (familiarly called The Saturday Reviler because of its reputation for acid criticism). Irked, she replied to the review, defending her book against the biased and uninformed reviewer who had so casually dismissed important contemporary authorities on the subject and then went on to challenge her thesis. This letter brought a further reply from the reviewer, continuing the attack on the book and including now the reputation of G. S. R. Mead, learned editor of *The Quest* and former officer of the Theosophical Society, whom she had cited as an authority on Gnostic texts. Other reviews were noteworthy. Nitze's appraisal for *Modern Language Review* was cordial but frank. She smarted under continued attack by the conservative Bruce and accused him of trying to discredit the character of her work, not because of an honest difference of opinion, but to promote his own theory of Christian origins of the Grail. He had misinterpreted her views, possibly the result of misreadings or her books or, worse still (she was not above the subtle cut) misreadings of the original texts or "summaries of texts."[49]

She had taken the ritual theory as far as she could. The dearth of texts remained an obstacle to further proofs, but the way lay open to Welsh scholars to continue Grail studies along the lines proposed in *From Ritual to Romance*. She was convinced that the source of Grail stories in the British Isles should be sought in the area of Pembrokeshire, Wales. Her interests were now moving to the *Perlesvaus* and the Welsh connections of that romance. Once again the battle of dates, priority, and traditional sources was on.[50]

---

[49] Weston thought that Ernst Brugger, "the best equipped of Arthurian scholars," would come over to her side and expected to convince him with *From Ritual to Romance*. Bad health prevented him from reviewing her book. The important German scholar Professor Samuel Singer told her his last doubts had been removed by her book. (Letter, February 29, 1920).

[50] Something more needs to be said of Frazer's age and the effects produced by *The Golden Bough* and similar works, including *From Ritual to Romance*. The encyclopedic accumulation of facts, so dear to the Victorian public, reported in an unhurried, poetical style speaks to latent uncertainty of where the new learning would lead. There is the Janus-like need of the age to escape from the past by returning to it and preserving it down to the last detail in books. Frazer paid a heavy price for knowledge, for it cost him his faith. The Christian God was merely the latest in a line of dying and reviving gods, and though he did not deal directly with the challenge to Christianity in print, the

A. E. Waite and The Quest

An exchange of barbed reviews stemming from opposing views of the literary qualities of an important romance and, in particular, its hero led to a minor feud between Weston and A. E. Waite, Rosicrucian, student of the Kabbalah and Freemasonry, officer of The Quest Society after it had broken away from the Theosophists. One source of the antagonism was their opposite views of the merits of the *Grand Saint Graal*. Weston had often expressed her dislike of the late romance; from a traditional standpoint it was the least interesting part of the Vulgate cycle. In fact, she

conclusion for him was inevitable. Yet he could lament the "deplorable skepticism of the age, as rationalism later turned into materialism. Weston's faith remained strong on the whole although she rejected Christocentrism, in part because vestiges of ancient ritual traceable to the Dying God clung to the worship of the second Person. Others, unable to return to the old faiths, sought other forms of comfort in occultist religions like Rosicrucianism, Freemasonry, Theosophy, and Spiritism. Weston commented on the spiritual emptiness of the 20s that drove men and women to these closet religions when their own church failed them. Other reactions were possible, even in unlikely places. Jane Harrison, for example, a long-time member of the Rationalist Society and a professed agnostic, confided to Gilbert Murray that she had had a mystical experience, but "I will never call it God – that name is defaced, but it is wonderful . . ." (Jessie G. Stewart, *Jane Ellen Harrison*, London, 1959, p. 113).

Weary of stupefying numbers of facts and Darwinian polemics, but unable to rebound from skepticism, many found in the myth of the Dying and Resurrected God a profound confirmation of faith. An instance of this involving C. S. Lewis and J. R. R. Tolkien is reported by Humphrey Carpenter in *The Inklings* (London, 1981, p. 44). Lewis was ridiculing the efficacy of Christ's death and resurrection. Tolkien replied that "pagan myths were, in fact, God expressing himself through the minds of poets, and using the image of their 'mythopoeia' to express fragments of his eternal truth. Well then, Christianity (he said) is exactly the same thing—with the enormous difference that the poet who invented it was God Himself, and the images He used were real men and actual history. Do you mean, asked Lewis, that the death and resurrection of Christ is the old 'dying god' story all over again? Yes, Tolkien answered, except that here is a *real* Dying God, with a precise location in history and definite historical consequences. The old myth had become a fact. But it still retains the character of a myth." Tolkien talked a little more of the way myth is to be enjoyed, "tasted," unlike less digestible abstract truths. The example convinced Lewis. As early as 1911, Robert Hugh Benson summarised the problem in *The Dawn of All* (London), pp. 33–4.

could barely conceal contempt for the Galahad quest altogether and specifically for the monkish character of the hero. From these opinions which she regularly vented within hearing distance of A. E. Waite, champion of the sublime Galahad, there arose a number of blistering attacks that continued even after Weston's death in the pages of his *The Holy Grail*, a massive compilation of Grail legends and learned commentary.[51] Waite held a strictly fideist view of the Grail and was therefore sympathetic to the Continental position on Christian origins, not for its literary or scholarly strength, but for the prominent place of sacramental religion in the major *Quest* romances.

Bulging with footnotes and appendices, Waite's *The Holy Grail* set its sights on Weston, leader of the ritualists, and less acerbically on Loomis as an apologist for the Celtic side. Waite admitted that no one had known the literature better than Weston, acknowledged her important reputation, but objected wholesale to her work from the "unreadable" verse translation of *Parzival* to the untenable ritual theory. His comments, often derisive, were aimed also at others who failed to see the fully Christian mystical meaning of the Grail, a view he held until his death in 1940. The main objection, personal and critical, to Weston was her relegating the Galahad quest to the last (thus declined) stage of Grail story development when the quest had passed out of the care of poets and into the hands of monks. To Waite, a mystic for whom the Grail was the most sacred hallow of Christianity, all other uses and interpretations incidental and irrelevant, Weston's handling of the subject missed the point; to treat Galahad as though he were a mere invention of priests, and a poorly conceived one at that, lacking as she often said in humanity and fallibility, misrepresented the Christian purpose of the entire Grail drama.

Actually, they had been at odds for years. *From Ritual to Romance* pre-empted his elucidation of the Tarot-Grail connection, and Waite was put out that Weston had failed to acknowledge his contributions on the subject (indeed, she had literally brushed aside his early book *The Hidden Church of the Holy Grail*, relegating him to a mere footnote). Also, the popularity of her book threatened to spread mistaken, even dangerous ideas of Grail origins, because of the use she had made of "cultist fictions." He resented and attacked as wrong the search by Weston and

---

51 Richard Cavendish, in an appendix to *King Arthur and the Grail* (New York, 1979), suggests that Weston published the Grail symbol-Tarot suit parallels as the result of contacts with Waite, "to the marked irritation of Waite" (p. 210). This may be so (Waite hints of her "forgetfulness"); however, Weston's notebooks contain no references to Waite at all while there are many notes on Falconnier's *Les XXII Lames Hermétiques du Tarot*, a standard work, and other related works cited in *From Ritual to Romance*.

her colleagues for pre-Christian sources when all the evidence pointed the other way. What after all were they really seeking but an anthropologist's (ultimately, the atheist's) unravelling of the Christian Mystery. Enlisted in this cause was Waite's good friend, the popular journalist and writer Arthur Machen. Machen, no doubt with Waite's blessing, offered his own version of Grail romance as an expanded and glorified Celtic ecclesiastical legend in a long essay "The Secret of the Sangraal." The introduction takes up the Nature cult hypothesis, brings into the discussion the books of Weston and Jane Harrison, and then by the use of irony and a leisurely appeal to common sense attempts to dispose of their favorite subject as well as the whole ritual theory. The "Covent Garden School of Anthropology" that spawned false interpretation then yields to Celtic sacramental symbolism.[52]

Waite, a recognised authority in all branches of esoteric philosophy, was an early member of the Order of the Golden Dawn. Believing himself the inheritor and guardian of the higher wisdom and dissatisfied that the Golden Dawn would not give up ritual magic and follow him into Christian mysticism, he made several attempts to take over the Order. When these failed, he began his own Temple, which attracted the eminent Evelyn Underhill, drawn by a promise of deeper mysticism (his Temple of Isis-Urania was to disappoint her); and Charles Williams, in whom the Golden Dawn and association with Waite would make profound and permanent change.[53] He joined The Quest Society, presided over by Weston's friend G. R. S. Mead, classicist, translator of Hermetic texts, former Theosophist. The Quest declared its object to be the promotion of comparative study of religion and philosophy "on the basis of experience"; its voice was the journal of articles, poems, and commentary on all experiences and events of a spiritual dimension. Among its members were Yeats, Algernon Blackwood, Rabindranath Tagore, John Masefield, Evelyn Underhill, and Ezra Pound. Waite's association with The Quest Society did not interfere with his strong opposition to Theosophy, probably because The Quest specialized in comparative religions and Western mysticism, Waite's sole interest, rather than the Eastern variety identified with the teachings of founder Mme Blavatsky.[54]

English occultists were either Theosophists (and members of break-

---

[52] In *The Shining Pyramid* (London, 1925), pp. 70–126. Andrew Lang was the first to use the expression "Covent Garden School of Anthropology" to describe the vegetation rite school of comparative religion because of the famed Covent Garden fruit and vegetable market.

[53] Francis King in *Ritual Magic in England* (London, 1970), p. 112.

[54] See Evelyn Underhill's interesting account of Waite's brand of occult Christian mysticism in her chapter "Mysticism and Magic," in *Mysticism* (London,

away groups like Mead's Quest Society), Freemasons, or independents. The first group worked through lectures and magazine articles (derisively described by a contemporary member of a rival sect as composed of "a large number of idle women who have the leisure to take a little occultism with their afternoon tea. Practically all the members are people with time and money").[55] Weston may have known MacGregor Mathers, one of the original members of the Golden Dawn, for he spent much time in Paris and London; certainly she knew of the notorious Aleister Crowley and the many ritualists, magicians, and spiritualists in occult centres like London and Paris (they were widespread in England, Scotland, France and Germany – and especially active in America).[56] Apart from her association with The Quest and its members (among whom no doubt there were many occultists) and communication with Yeats and other members of the Golden Dawn whose knowledge she drew upon and welcomed, there is no reason to seek her deeper involvement with occultists. Her name comes up nowhere else but in the published lists of the Quest Society. Though most members of occult groups preferred to remain anonymous, secrecy of the ritual, not the membership, was the inviolable rule. Weston herself observed with regret that the materialism of her day had forced many into occultism and other desperate associations – hardly a sympathetic comment. That she found interesting unusual phenomena like the stigmata, prescience, auto-suggestion, etc., is not surprising in one so well-read and cosmopolitan, one so steeped in curious lore and popular superstition. Also, such things as interested occultists were "all the rage" as well among the general public early in the century as the potential of the human mind even to delude itself came under greater scrutiny.

At the very time Weston was deploring the proliferation of occult groups (in the aftermath of World War I rapidly filling with people in search of a faith), the rituals and ancient traditions of the movement were suffering debasement at the hands of new members who misapplied the rituals and did not know or plainly misunderstood the esoteric meanings behind them. This was so serious a challenge to the continued existence of the Order of the Golden Dawn, that those few remaining adepts who possessed the knowledge began to publish the rituals later for fear that

1911; reprinted New York, 1961), pp. 149–164. Waite's piety and pedantry (rivers of learning loosed mercilessly) are touched on in King's *Ritual Magic*, pp. 94–5, 175–95. He was quite intolerant of other points of view. Underhill relied on J. L. W. for folklore derivations.

[55] King, p. 103.
[56] Crowley's antics were highly visible: for five guineas the public could witness his re-enactment of the mystic Rites of Eleusis in a darkened, incense-laden Caxton Hall. King describes the spectacle (pp. 115–17).

they would disappear altogether.[57] Waite, however, was motivated in his books by the high purpose of exposing false gods and wasted devotion; ritual was worth preserving only as it served the Christian mystic to achieve entry into the Mysteries.

But it was not in the pages of *The Quest* that Waite assessed her interpretation of the Grail Mysteries. That was left to editor Mead, not only as a respectful gesture to the important Weston, but because Waite (clearly the most capable to review the Grail from the sacramental point of view) would be hostile to her book from first to last. When Waite finally went to print in *The Holy Grail* (subtitled "The Galahad Quest in Arthurian Literature"), he accused her rather colourfully of being the dupe of liars and mountebanks, of being fed so-called secrets of the Tarot and initiation rites by fakes and imposters. He never mentions her participation or membership in any groups or occult societies (surely he would not have lost the opportunity to damn both her and the cults in one sweep were it possible), but speaks only of her gullibility, of her habit of hearing only that which she wanted to hear (and didn't those frauds who humored her know it!). He discounted the evidence she had produced; of course, for him to admit any of her theory would damage his claim to the true Christian interpretation of Grail romances. All this he put into print after her death as part of a massive assault on her reputation.

The quarrel between them surfaced in 1909 with Waite's *Quest* review of *The Legend of Sir Perceval*. He rejected the work on grounds of misinterpretation of the Grail and Grail hero. In reply, Weston questioned his admitted prejudices against any interpretation of the Grail other than Christian; she asked if he truly believed, as he said, that only "under the Christian dispensation alone did man seek after God and find Him." Did he really hold that a pre-Christian or non-Christian search for God was worthless? She defended her work against his charge of irrational or inconsequential arguments; every one of the features attached to the story was capable of rational explanation to a reader with an *open* mind. She noted full well his open contempt for folklore, his scorn for Gawain as a Grail hero because of that hero's many amorous encounters, and his disregard for the opinions of internationally recognised critics as well as for the evidence of texts. Did he even know the texts? The tone of the reply is typical of ironic Weston: disdainful but controlled, filled with genteel contempt for Waite's hero Galahad and the favoured *Grand Saint Graal*. The first she disliked, the other detested. Waite's knowledge was only partial, she said; thus some errors were inevitable, but some errors were inexcusable, particularly those that had disfigured his own *The*

---

[57] See King, pp. 154–57.

Hidden Church of the Grail (Bruce later dismissed the work with a single phrase: "a fantastic book"), which he had written for an uncritical audience with little first-hand knowledge of texts.

Waite came back with a shrill defence, falling back upon his Christian position in all matters. To argue texts was irrelevant. He took satisfaction after her death in associating Tarot divination "with Occult Sects of Miss Weston's type," in connecting her interpretations snidely to "her Fertility complex," and hinting that he, not she, had been the first to notice the symbolism of the Tarot trumps. The "fertility" phrase obliquely refers to Bruce's chapter heading "Miss Weston's Gawain-Complex," and, of course, to the suppressed sexual urges in the spinster's life, a point of humor not reserved to Waite and his circle once she identified the phallic symbolism of the Tarot Cups and Swords. Waite's anti-Weston polemic does little credit to him, and the reader may speculate what heat would have steamed out of this debate had Waite spoken out this way while she lived.

Wagner and Weston

Richard Wagner's music, the Bayreuth festivals, the rich materials of myth and folklore from which he drew, all inspired Weston's first scholarly effort, the translation of Wolfram's *Parzival*, with notes by Weston and Alfred Nutt. The attraction of Wagner's innovative music was so widespread in Europe it is hardly surprising that the literary folklorist especially should want to mine the Germanic myths dramatised in the *Ring* cycle. As a young man Wagner had been charmed by Grimm's *Deutsche Mythologie*; later he would see in myth the embodiment of the culture-spirit of the people (he would say race), and as such myth was a useful vehicle of social regeneration. His poetic way of joining myth and music stirred an army of admirers. Jessie Weston was among them. She recognised the public's need to look into the past (even of Germanic "barbarism," as Gibbon put it), and so set about bringing the original legends Wagner had reworked into operas to British readers. She had studied music at the conservatory in Hildesheim in the opening years of Wagner frenzy, and lived in Paris where enthusiasm was almost as intense as in his native land. There were the Wagner societies and yearly pilgrimages to Bayreuth, a meeting place of sorts also for fellow medievalists where work in progress was often discussed. She wrote of one of these visits that Alfred Nutt suggested she translate Wolfram's poem as a way of making Wagner's sources available to the public. Two years later with the publication of *Parzival*, her career as a translator was launched. Also begun was a long association with Alfred Nutt's publishing firm. The book was well received, and again with the public in mind, she wrote a small book on *Lohengrin* and then produced the more ambitious *Legends of the Wagner Drama*, a full account of tales from the *Nibelungenlied* and *Volsungasaga* used by Wagner in the *Ring*. She included here her personal favourite *Parzival*, and *Tristan und Isolde*, which she claimed for the British by "inherited right." There is little mystery in her elucidations, no philosophy, no trace of social Darwinism evident in Wagner's own writings, only an unembarrassed love of heroic saga. A sense of the age is there in the title she gives herself as author: "By One of the Folk," she writes, a naive homage to *Volkskunde* as conceived by the artist, a romantic exalting of the nameless noble "folkloristic" bard. She often remarked on Wagner's genius, yet she was not blind to narrative faults, particularly where Wagner's tampering with original conceptions of character and motivation debased the exalted purposes of the original. An idealism higher than Wagner's lay behind her comments on the maestro's judgment.

Weston's interest in Wagner was part of the tide sweeping England and the continent in the last quarter of the century, a Wagnermania that united artists and intellectuals in a common transport of emotion. She was hardly alone. Swinburne, the Rossettis, George Moore, Hardy, Galsworthy, Shaw, Arnold Bennett – pre-Raphaelites, esthetes, naturalist novelists, all became "perfect Wagnerites" for a time at least. The Word had been brought to England's shores by Franz Hueffer, friend of the influential Ford Madox Brown who introduced Hueffer to his circle of writer and artists friends already stirred by the uses French Symbolist poets were making of Wagner's music theory. When Hueffer became music editor of *The Times* the effects spilled over to the public at large.[58] The Wagner Society was founded (Weston was an early member of the *Wagnerverein*), and before long Londoners could attend a "Wagner Night at Covent Garden."[59]

All this may seem remote from her later work. However, Weston's

---

[58] Jacques Barzun, *Darwin, Freud, Wagner* (New York, 1943; reprinted New York, 1958), pp. 286–96. Barzun gives a fascinating account of the Wagner phenomenon (pp. 283–96). He sums up, "Bohemians, decadents, bourgeois, socialists, and other-worldly enthusiasts merged their differences in a frenzy of love and adoration." Shaw's homage in "The Perfect Wagnerite" is well known. Devotion among the French was even more intense. Among Wagner enthusiasts were Zola, Huysmans, and of course the Symbolists Baudelaire, Mallarmé, Verlaine, etc., for whom Wagner's music was inspiration.

[59] The Wagner Society, founded in the 1870s, flourished around the turn of the century, and disappeared by 1910. Not all was rosy, however. Early critical

commentary on Wagner has passed into modern musical criticism in so unexpected a way as to underscore her continuing effect even outside Arthurian studies: on the sensibilities of Wagner lovers. From Ernest Newman's appreciative review of her translations and analyses of plot in *Wagner Nights* (1949) to an article in the Metropolitan's *Opera News* (April 1982) summarizing and applying Weston's ritual theory to the Metropolitan's production of *Parsifal*, her stamp on Wagner literature is continuing. Not always admired, sometimes damned, she hangs on to worry some critics sixty-five years after her death because she has impudently questioned the master's revisionism. For instance, Deryck Cooke in *I Saw the World End* quotes Weston extensively for the succinctness of her commentary, but contemptuously dismisses her moral judgments of *Siegfried*.[60] Weston objected to Sieglinde's conduct and found the behavior of Siegmund and Sieglinde reprehensible, a violation of epic and moral codes. Cooke responds to this, "It should not really be necessary to answer 'moral' strictures of this outmoded kind," then proceeds to answer in spite of himself: "Miss Weston's views only too obviously belong to a time – the eighteen-nineties – when the rights of women were as yet hardly thought of; when adultery, especially by a woman, was regarded as a disgrace; and when incest between brother and sister – even if they met as strangers – was something unmentionable. Wagner, of course, was dramatising a revolutionary condemnation of these hidebound Victorian ideas." There is certainly nothing Victorian left in Cooke. He also finds it necessary to deliver a seven-page rebuttal of her analysis of *The Valkyrie*, noting her use of the phrase "passion of love" with an ironic "Perhaps Miss Weston did not regard love as a passion" – a minor but telling indication of how the sexless spinster may be as empty of a real emotion as the adoring Wagnerite is of charm. Even in a permissive age Wagner is hardly the model of right conduct and soaring idealism. Jousting with Jessie Weston's spectre eighty-five years after publication of her little book creates its own little drama of survival. She was not a Perfect Wagnerite.

reaction in London could be harsh. *Tristan und Isolde* was called rankly offensive in its first London production in 1882. Nevertheless, by the time of Wagner's death in 1883 Wagner's importance was everywhere acknowledged. Perhaps few today except the most ardent Wagnerites would go so far as to agree with a recent comment by Reginald Goodall, distinguished conductor of the English National Opera, that Wagner's was "possibly the greatest mind of the nineteenth century." *Wagner*, N.S. 2 (1981), p. 12.

[60] She named specifically "treachery, violation of the marital bed and guest-rights." See *I Saw the World End* (Oxford, 1979), pp. 305, 307–8, 315–16.

Life After From Ritual to Romance

In 1920 Jessie Weston received the Rose Mary Crawshaw prize of the British Academy and a "very acceptable" £100. This she put towards the cost of cataract surgery. The rigors of *From Ritual to Romance* had strained her already failing eyesight and she admitted that finishing the book was very difficult. In 1923 she was made Doctor of Literature by the University of Wales, the supreme honour of her long career, "on the ground of the distinction of her work on the Arthurian romance." Mary Williams, then professor of French Literature, presented her to the university with these words:

> I venture to believe that no one, be it man or woman, is better known on the Continent as well as in these islands for her studies in the domain of Arthurian romance. Her researches have ever been prosecuted with that patience, zeal and love of the truth which are characteristic of the great scholar. At a time when the Arthurian legend was receiving but scant attention in this country she devoted her great learning to this subject and broke much new ground, which has made it possible for others to follow her. Our debt to her as Welshmen is greater than we yet realise, for she is the first to have suggested the role Wales played in the formation of the romantic aspect of the Grail story, and she has contributed more than any other towards the elucidation of the very baffling problems of the true significance of the Grail legend.[61]

She delivered a long speech on the major Arthurian romances that could reasonably stand as a short course in the subject; it was thorough and entertaining and everywhere radiated her great talent for bringing her subject to every kind of audience. Mary Williams liked it enough to handwrite a copy that ran twenty-two pages. Henceforth, Jessie L. Weston was Dr Weston.

But 1923 also brought dislocation. For years she had kept an apartment on the Rue de la Ville l'Evêque in the fashionable 8è arrondissement. Her books, furniture, valuables were there. Visits to her sister's home in

---

[61] From the address to the Congregation, July 21, 1923. There was similar praise from Sidney Hartland in *Y Cymmrodor* of 1921 for a "triumph of patience, learning, and sagacity. A secret which has been kept for seven hundred years has at length been unveiled by her wise and persistent researches. The records of those researches, crowned with *From Ritual to Romance*, will stand as a permanent monument to the greatness of her achievement. In explaining the famous tale she has added beyond denial another glory to Welsh romance" (p. 59).

Carshalton, to Brighton or Bournemouth (less frequent now), travels across Europe, always brought her back to Paris. This was her home, and here she intended to spend the rest of her days. Now, on a wave of anti-English sentiment and a new venality, she was forced to give up her apartment. To renew a lease, she complained, one had to bribe the concièrge; even then, only quarterly renewals were possible. She found Parisian life much changed, demoralising, and prepared to come home to England for good. She secured a four-year lease on a flat in Biddulph Mansions in the Maida Vale section of London, hired a cook and live-in housekeeper (such a staff as she had kept in Paris), and plunged into her work once more.

There was much left to do: articles for *Romania*, *Modern Philology*, and other journals, including the increasingly important *The Quest*, and of course there was the *Perlesvaus* book. Also in 1923 she was at work on "Literary Cycles of the Middle Ages," a long chapter for Volume VI of the *Cambridge Mediaeval History*. Nitze wrote her that Bruce had just died – she speaks with regret of that loss on the heels of Schofield and the French Arthurian Huet, an old colleague in Celtic studies and the reviewer of *From Ritual to Romance* for *Le Moyen Age*. "The ranks are thinning," she told Mary Williams. It was up to the young to take up the cause.

Yet she had a cause or two left in her, particularly where her church and her conscience collided. As an Anglican, she followed very closely the policies and politics of the Church of England, and now felt compelled to speak against the church's neglect to teach adequately its basic creeds, just as a decade before she had spoken out against conciliatory treatment of Germany, the land she had known well now hateful to her. The issue was a religious one, the growing Christocentrism within the church, a deepening interest in England in the relics of Christian worship, in the Mass and the "monstrance," such as she had seen everywhere in Europe and thanked God England free of. The scholar steeped in centuries of folklore and superstition, an outspoken adherent of ritual theory vitalized by the recurrent drama of the Dying and Resurrected God, a traveller ever observant of the remains of ancient customs clinging to, even shaping, religious practice of European nations, she distrusted the turn away from worship of the Holy Spirit to the Person of Christ. A surge of 1920s ecumenism proclaiming a unified Christendom alarmed her. It was founded on illusion, she wrote. She refused to look back to a so-called "ideal past," the rosy picture of a "Merrie Olde England" pre-Reformation style that some uninformed Anglicans were preaching. (Weston was not a sentimentalist about the Middle Ages. Almost any other age was better lived in but not studied.) She rejected the "wildly fantastic" suggestions of noted churchmen that reunion with the Roman Church would return Europe to an idyllic age of the imagination that had never existed; she denounced the "glowing . . . picture of a Catholic Europe" that never was, being painted by men ignorant of the cruelties of life in medieval times.

The Westons had produced and would continue to produce distinguished churchmen; her nephew Frank Weston, the Bishop of Zanzibar, already celebrated for his defiance of the Germans in East Africa, was now embroiled in a doctrinal controversy within the Church of England. Speaking forthrightly was a duty, and arguing her convictions was as natural to Jessie Weston in religious matters as in Arthurian criticism. The strength of the English character she attributed to a love of truth and duty instilled through knowledge of moral law in the Scriptures, particularly the Old Testament. Lying was abhorrent to her, however worthy the reason for the lie. She was fond of pointing out that French friends throught this a "peculiarly English" trait: "Vous avez plus de conscience." She deplored the scant attention being paid in churches to lessons and epistles in the eagerness to get to the Mass. Reminding her readers of the debt Christians owed to Jews, she remarked that one reason anti-Semitism had found till then no firm footing in England as it had among continental Catholics was precisely that the Romanists knew nothing of the Bible except for the Gospels; thus the Jew is the villain of the "great Drama of the Passion." "This anti-Semitism," she wrote, "is in his blood and the manifestations, not always spectacular as in pogroms or the Dreyfus case, are sad and chronic."[62]

Fearful of the trend to ecumenism, she aimed her charges at the *Church Times*, the influential weekly organ of the Church of England, which she accused (1) of falling to the pro-Romanist faction, and (2) of anti-Jewish bias in their criticisms of British policy in Palestine and "in sweeping attacks on the Jews as a whole – as inspirers of the Bolshevik attacks on Christianity and civilization in general." She warned her readers that the determined minority had as its goal "nothing less than *submission* to Rome." A final warning alludes to events already under way in Europe whose full and horrifying consequences she did not live to see: "We know in politics the danger of such minorities who know their own minds, imposing their will upon a larger, well-meaning, but more 'nebulous' minded body." Aging had toughened her will without diminishing foresight. The article written about 1927 and destined for publication in *The Quest* (now her polemics publisher) never appeared in print. It was too controversial and probably did not reflect the attitudes of some of the membership of the society.

---

[62] "Quo Vadis: Some Reflections Upon the Anglo-Catholic Movement," an unpublished essay signed Dr Ignotas.

Had she thought of herself as unique, as more than a patient, sometimes plodding worker disentangling lovely knots, she would have been satisfied with the success of *From Ritual to Romance*, and perhaps settled in to write her *memoirs*, as Jane Harrison was doing. She holds an important place in the history of Arthurian scholarship, and her ritual theory has been very far-reaching in ways she could not have expected. Also, hers was an exemplary life of achievement in the face of prejudice against women, overt and subtle. Perhaps that made her more defiant of accepting submission to her critics. She came against an entrenched group of European academics who claimed exclusive right to Arthurian studies, a claim bolstered by decades of distinguished scholarship in all fields, and she was not intimidated. Courtesies usually observed among scholars who disagreed dissolved into ironies or worse. Her so-called "intractable" opposition to the German faction grew out of repeated attacks by the abrasive Foerster and Golther, the arch-apologists of Chrétien's priority. Also vexing to those who wished her silent were her Celtic views inherited from Gaston Paris and Alfred Nutt, old adversaries of the German philologists. Furthermore, within the criticism lay the sub-text of distrust of theories insisted upon by Miss Jessie L. Weston of London and Bournemouth. She was a woman and English besides, striding confidently into an arena long dominated by German men. That she remained firm and overcame the bias against the woman scholar as fully equal and productive is evident by the stature attained in her lifetime, the more striking in that she did not have a university behind her.

She began her career as a translator, poet, and taleteller, a romantic occupation suitable for a dreamy Victorian maiden of forty-four raised on the exploits of General Gordon in the Sudan and Burton on the Nile, on the otherworldliness of the pre-Raphaelites and Tennyson. But she was not true to type. She did not follow the ordinary course of respectable marriage and motherhood; this she owed to her parents' recognizing exceptional potential in the child Jessie and providing for European rather than English training. Her education abroad, years spent away from the family, matured her quickly and made travelling from one country to another second nature. The purported Victorian delicacy of constitution that kept young ladies sheltered and submissive did not exist for her. A continental education gave her poise, endurance, and the confidence to insist that her English voice be heard wherever Arthurians assembled.

She had often to deal with mismanaged compliments: a reviewer tells his readers that Miss Jessie Weston "has a hobby" – he refers to her interest in Grail literature.[63] Sometimes with personal slights: a reader

[63] The reviewer writing in *The Expository Times* (October, 1920) is at once

sarcastically glosses a passage in his copy of *The Legend of Sir Lancelot* – "And what would Miss Jessie know about love?"[64] A woman, a spinster – say or think what they liked, she was too important to care, and by now too old.

Her success is noteworthy in another respect too. She was not an academic. She had come to her reputation without the peculiar distinction conferred by university affiliation; she was always just outside the preferred circle. There were other non-academics in the field, certainly, men like Sidney Hartland lawyer and Alfred Nutt businessman, but these were men gainfully employed pursuing a novel avocation. To what institution or person had she to answer except the critics? She was respectful of rank and degree, and included the academic title of critics cited in support of her position (so, Professor von Schroeder or Professor Singer; on the other hand, merely Foerster or Hoffmann). She was flattered when asked to speak to college students. She liked young people, and often received the aspiring Arthurian in her home. When in 1923 she became Jessie L. Weston, D. Litt., she wore the title with pride and some modesty, still sensitive to the academy's exclusiveness, but satisfied that formal recognition of her achievements was complete.

Why Jessie Weston more than any other scholar while she lived and long after she died excites warm reaction on both sides of a question cannot be easily explained. True, she pushed her way into a man's world, whether of Arthurian romance or Wagnerian opera, and was resented publicly or privately, but none could dispute her learning or knowledge of the texts at the time. She worked hard and steadily at elucidating the fabric of romance from the two perspectives of medievalist and folklorist.

indulgent and gentlemanly: "Miss Jessie L. Weston has a hobby. It is worthy of a woman and a scholar. It has an interest that is poetical, romantic, religious, and even scientific." Such patronizing was rare but indicative of attitudes of her day, which even scholarship did not dispel in all cases.

64 Once, Alfred Nutt handed her a copy of *The Legend of Sir Lancelot* belonging to a friend of his, Robert Steele, who had written a running commentary critical of the book. His comments were scribbled page after page in the margins. She pencilled in an answer to each point, ending with a long note tucked in at the back utterly demolishing his claims to know the texts. When Steele to his horror learned what Nutt had done, he affixed an apologetic letter to his own copy explaining his intentions and returned it to his shelves. His embarrassment was probably caused by several notes alluding to the maidenly Miss Weston. In one instance she claimed shallowness of Lancelot and Guenevere's love. To which he added: "Perhaps Miss Weston is not an expert in these matters." To which she replied: "I know the real article from a sham, that's all.'

To her critics, what was conviction in others was in her obstinacy; what was in others independence was in her wilfulness; what in them speculation, in her groundless adventurism. She had proven herself more than a match for the scholars who would tolerate the lady's dabbling in local legends and folkways, but not in the serious questions of literary provenance. The sheer boldness of her method invited debate, as we have seen. That she was a spinster gave legitimacy to a life dedicated to scholarship, but raised the usual doubts about how well she understood the romantic passions and attachments of literary characters – questions certainly never posed to male scholars.

She held her own in a highly competitive intellectual circle and for a time her ideas eclipsed those of others in the field. She never stood aside from an argument, and when provoked let fly spirited barbs that sharpened as she grew older; so that by 1925 she spoke of Lot's "embarrassing retreat," Bruce's "extraordinarily feeble" argument brought into "amusing relief" by his contradictions and inconsistencies, and the "hasty and superficial treatment" of a work by these two scholars. Her fondness for Wagner and Germanic myth have been interpreted in hindsight as sympathy for the Aryan racial myth – a false, undeserved slur. Anyone familiar with her anti-German pamphlets deploring the notion of national destiny, or cultural supremacy as an excuse to justify war and its attendant atrocities will know the truth of the matter. For good or ill, she disliked Germans; there is no evidence of her having returned to Germany after the Hildesheim days except for the Bayreuth festival concerts though she speaks often of travel to other countries across Europe. Scattered through her notebooks are telling comments omitted later in published versions – small asides better left out. Reacting to the assertion that the German national character improved medieval knighthood, she writes, "If this were really so we may well exclaim mournfully that *quantum mutatum ab illo!*" In a comment in an article on the *Perlesvaus* she is repelled by the ugly sabre scar young Germans sport as a sign of manhood, as if that were all one needed. Her treatment by German critics has already been dealt with. It should be possible for Weston to admire Germanic myth and Wagnerian opera and to express the intellectual enthusiasms of the time (especially strong in comparative folklore), without the burden of association with myths of Aryan supremacy, an arrogance she repeatedly attacked.

In 1927 she agreed to review Roger Sherman Loomis's book and looked forward to a visit by Loomis and Laura Hibbard in early September.[65] She

---

[65] Helaine Newstead recalled that Loomis mentioned that he and Laura Hibbard had paid a call. Weston and Loomis corresponded, but their letters have not survived.

had just returned from a three-month stay on the continent, with most of the time spent in Kandersteg, a summer resort near Berne, and a shorter visit to her beloved Paris. Though her permanent residence was London, clearly she felt quite at home in France and Switzerland.

Despite a convalescence following major surgery, she worked steadily on *Perlesvaus*, received friends and family regularly, and kept active for her 77 years. There was the one last book left to do. We recall that she had written *From Ritual to Romance* despite blinding cataracts, but now she was ten years older and ill. In June of 1928 she was again in France for the summer. She wrote to Hope Emily Allen (whom she knew by reputation only) from Evian-les-Bains inviting her to Biddulph Mansions in August when she planned to return home, but by that time, stricken with cancer, her health had begun to sink rapidly.

On September 29, 1928, in her 78th year, she died of complications following surgery, and was buried in a perishable coffin, as she had requested, in Carshalton, near London, where she had spent much time at the home of her sister Edith and favorite niece Mabel.[66]

There were no provisions made for publication of *Perlesvaus*. No doubt she fully expected to finish this, her last work. It lacked several chapters covering the events of two branches (though with the exception of an identification of Brian des Illes with a historical figure, by which she expected to prove conclusively the early date of the romance, only the folklore segments and whatever other traditional elements could be used to prove the priority of the *Perlesvaus* over the *Queste* would have interested her); and several chapters were in a first-draft state, unnumbered and uncorrected. This was the work to round off her career, summing up the research activity of the 1920s with solutions to the most problematic prose romance in Arthurian literature. The book would have been a valuable middle step at a time when serious study of the *Perlesvaus* was underway (Nitze's edition would not appear for several years yet), and many of her insights and conclusions were still incubating in the minds of other scholars whose contributions were to come later. At the least, publication would have moved the ever-widening Arthurian circle to lively debate once again.

The biographer must now apologize for the faults of omission. Instead of a cache of letters or diaries that reveal the private side of what to the

---

[66] She had barely finished revisions of a full set of articles for the *Encyclopaedia Britannica* and the bibliography for the *Cambridge Mediaeval History*, neither of which had been posted, when death came. Apparently she expected to resume work after the usual period of post-surgical convalescence, and so left no instructions.

public was a rich, stimulating life, one finds mere bits and pieces remaining from which to create a fair sketch of a fascinating woman. Sixty-five years brings a great silence. All who knew Jessie Weston have died, and gone are the countless notes and letters she jotted off routinely filled with details personal and professional that would have given a complete sense of her. For many, she is destined to live on as a shadowy figure behind the Waste Land theme thanks to the modern poet, who has acknowledged the use of her work, but her influence extends far beyond a single poem or single scholarly work into the imagination and creative energy of several generations of students of literature, mythology, and comparative religion.[67] Her great strength was not the case laid out with absolute precision

[67] In August 1954, T. S. Eliot was informed by the Cambridge Press of the many requests over the years for a new printing of *From Ritual to Romance* and asked if he would write a preface or introduction. The feeling in the firm was that the book would serve as a reference for Eliot's *The Waste Land*. Eliot replied he enthusiastically endorsed a reissue, noting that Faber had considered reprinting, but his colleagues decided such a venture would not be commercially profitable. "It is a tantalising book and leaves one with a curiosity as to where the author's further researches would have led her had she lived. May I ponder on the matter of a preface? I am not convinced that I am the right man for the job. I have no reputation as an anthropologist, and I fear that a preface from me would tie the book up too closely with my own exploitation of it, and therefore do Miss Weston an injustice." Eliot promised to think the matter over. In November he wrote that an introduction by him would be inappropriate. In 1955 Faber and Faber expressed interest in reprinting, but CUP had by then leased rights to Doubleday, who put out 25,000 copies with 500 hard-cover copies issued simultaneously by Peter Smith. In 1960 they issued another 25,000 copies. An Italian-language edition was planned in 1959, and in 1970 a Polish translation was in preparation. By that time, CUP regretted having given up the rights. The book was part of history by then, and may or may not have led, as one of the Syndics feared, "to people talking dangerously about literature" (Memo, March 2, 1965). Recent T. S. Eliot scholars have held opposing opinions on the poet's use of Weston, particularly her description of the Tarot. Some claim A. E. Waite or Eliot's "occult connections" to be the chief source of *The Waste Land* in spite of his statement in the famous endnotes. An account of conflicting views of critics about Weston's "occultism" and its influence on Eliot and modern poetry is given in Leon Surette's "The Waste Land and Jessie Weston: A Reassessment," (*Twentieth Century Literature*, 33 (1987), 223–43).

A recent appearance occurred in the film *Apocalypse Now*. The camera moves slowly to Kurtz's table to linger on two books, Frazer's *The Golden Bough*, and lying on it, *From Ritual to Romance*. So much for subtlety. *From Ritual to Romance* no doubt will continue to turn up in unlikely places.

and verifiable evidence; often she relied on insight into the heart of the thing and instinctive judgments to guide her argument to an appointed end, convinced that in the absence of contrary evidence, that was where the truth or the solution lay. She was not afraid to speak her mind and never stood to the side of controversy.

If she lived in romance tradition at all, it was as the respectful observer, never confusing the starkly different age that produced that literature with her own age, preferable in every way. Like other scholars of her time – Lang, Rhys, Kittredge, Nutt, Paton – she was dedicated to understanding folkways and faiths that more than war and dry statistics define culture and whatever lies deeper in the human spirit – a sense of the heroic and delight in the Mystery.

APPENDIX I

WORKS BY JESSIE L. WESTON

Parzival. 2 Vols. London, 1894.

Wolfram von Eschenbach's poem translated into English for the first time; appendices on Angevin allusions, Wolfram's sources, Wolfram and Chrétien.

Lohengrin: Fifty Years After. London, 1895.

Subtitled, "by one of the folk," a retelling of the legend in ballad form.

The Rose Tree of Hildesheim and Other Poems. London, 1896.

Contains title poem (a long narrative poem about the legendary rose bush in the chancel of the cathedral); *Knights of King Arthur's Court*, composed of short lyrics "Sir Gawayne," "Sir Tristan," "Sir Perceval," "Sir Lancelot"; *Songs*, short, imagistic love lyrics "Saint Valentine," "Sunset Dreams," "One Year"; dramatic lyrics, "Easter Eve" and "A Christmas Carol."

The Legend of Sir Gawain. London, 1897; New York, 1972.

In this first study of Arthurian legend, Weston finds existing side by side with Chrétien's stories of Arthur another body of tales deriving from source very much like Chrétien's but fuller in detail; parallels between Cuchulainn and Gawain and other evidence of Irish origins; an "other-world" adventure (Chateau Merveil) rather than Grail Castle formed part of Gawain's story early in legend's development.

Legends of the Wagner Drama. London, 1898; New York: 1978.

Containing the stories of the Nibelungen, Parsifal, Lohengrin, Tristan and Isolde, Tannhaüser.

"*Ywain and Gawain* and *Le Chevalier au Lion*," MQLL, 1 (1898), 98–107, 194–201.

A close comparison of the fourteenth-century English poem and Chrétien's *Le Chevalier au Lion* concluding that *Ywain* takes some parts from source other than Chrétien and that the *Mabinogion* "Lady of the Fountain" derives from source earlier than Chrétien, contrary to current critical opinion.

King Arthur and His Knights. London, 1899.

Examination of Arthurian romance for general audiences.

Sir Gawain and the Green Knight. Vol. 2 in Arthurian Romances Unrepresented in Malory. London, 1899; New York, 1972.

A prose rendering with introductory essay and endnotes; the first in the ARUM series translating many little known romances.

Tristan and Iseult. 2 Vols. Vol. 2 in ARUM. London, 1899; New York, 1972.

Gottfried's version freely rendered with conclusion supplied by poem of Heinrich von Freiburg; essay and notes.

Guingamor, Lanval, Tyolet, Le Bisclaveret. Vol. 3 in ARUM. London, 1900; New York, 1972.

Four lais of Marie de France in prose translation; essay and notes.

The Soul of a Countess. London, 1900.

Short stories including title story, a well crafted, effective prose narrative of the animating of a wood-spirit for whom a human soul is sought; "The Sorrow of the King," a tale of the journey of the Wise Men; "Our Lady of the Forest," a Miracle of the Virgin set in a remote time; "The Unknown Master," a short tale of a boy's love of nature and song; "The Last Valkyr," in which Wotan's old religion confronts the new Christianity; "The Archbishop That Was a Saint," a simple moral tale.

Morien. Vol. 4 in ARUM. London, 1901; New York, 1972.

Translation of the quest part of the unique Dutch metrical version of the *Lancelot*; essay and notes.

"Correspondence: 'The Golden Bough': Moab or Edom," *F–L*, 12 (1901), 347.

A note on Sir James Frazer's citation of Kings 3:27 as instance of substitute sacrifice of son for father. Weston doubts this can be fairly quoted to support his argument because of the misreading of grammatical construction.

Review of *The Wife of Bath's Tale: Sources and Analogues*, by Howard Maynadier, *F–L*, 12 (1901), 373–74.

Weston concurs with the main idea of a lost Celtic original of Loathly Lady tale, but offers these points: 1) the question motif is of Northern influence; 2) the tale should be connected with Gawain as Celtic rather than Arthurian hero. Suggests Maynadier's "lost English source" be replaced by earlier form of *The Marriage of Sir Gawain*, derived from an Irish source.

The Romance of Charlemagne and His Peers. London, 1901; New York, 1972.

A survey of the *chansons de geste*.

The Legend of Sir Lancelot du Lac. London, 1901; New York, 1972.

Study of the *Lanzelet* of Ulrich von Zatzikhoven, the "cerf au pied blanc" episode of the Dutch Lancelot; Chrétien's *Charrette*, and the prose *Lancelot* with resulting attack on Foerster's theory of Chrétien as an original writer and strong case made for insular origins of his romances.

The Three Days' Tournament. London, 1902; New York, 1965.

Study of the Lancelot episode; this is an appendix to *LSL*, above.

Sir Cleges and Sir Libeaus Desconus. Vol. 5 in ARUM. London, 1902; New York, 1972.

Translation of two English metrical romances; essay and notes.

Review of *Studies in the Fairy Mythology in Arthurian Romance*, by Lucy A. Paton, *F–L*, 14 (1903), 437–43.

Concedes this is a valuable study but objects to this: regarding Morgain Le Fay as of pure Celtic fairy origin, to a Morgain-Morrigan connection, to the use of the Huth-*Merlin* and Malory to show origins. Rivalry between Morgain ad Guenevere is of very early date; Morgain is a loan from Scandinavian mythology. The Grail Sword recalls Wieland.

Sir Gawain at the Grail Castle. Vol. 6 in ARUM. London, 1903; New York, 1972.

Translation of three episodes recounting Gawain's visit to the Grail Castle: versions of Wauchier, Heinrich von dem Türlin's *Diu Crône*, and prose *Lancelot*; essay and notes.

"Waucher de Denain and the Prologue of the Mons MS.," *R*, 32 (1904), 333–43.

There is agreement between some parts of the "Elucidation" of the Mons MS. of the *Perceval* and Wauchier's account of Perceval's visit to the Grail Castle that points to a common source in a body of poems dealing with Gawain's deeds. Both cite Bleheris as their authority. Bleheris contributed short tales to Arthurian lore which Wauchier and others used in a purer form than the author of the "Elucidation." Gawain is probably the original hero of Grail legend, a traditional story rather than a literary invention.

"Wauchier de Denain and Bleheris," *R*, 34 (1905), 100–5

MS. B.M. 36614 proves the Welsh birth of Bleheris, strengthening his identification with Bledhericus, the "famosus ille fabulator" of Giraldus Cambrensis. The Count of Poitiers, who heard this story from Bleheris, is identified as William VIII (d. 1137), father of Eleanor and Bleheris" patron. The problem of which language William knew the story in persists. Original extensive collection of tales by Bleheris must have existed in literary form before Chrétien; Gawain was the hero of that collection.

"The Scoppo del Carro at Florence," *F–L*, 16 (1905), 182–84.

In the Easter ceremony of the "Scoppo," elaborately decorated oxen draw the "Carro," a decorated urn-like erection, to the Piazza del Duomo, where a pillar wreathed with fireworks is set afire in expectation of igniting the "Carro," – all symbolizing augury of good harvest.

"A Note on the Legend of Merlin," *F–L*, 16 (1905), 182–84.

Disputes Gaster's theory that the prose romances preceded and thus were the source of the poetical, that the author of the *Grand Saint Graal* and *Queste* was a monk. Concedes that Merlin's birth story is not specifically insular, but world-wide, and very old.

"Correspondence: 'The Legend of Merlin'," *F–L*, 17 (1906), 230–31.

This note citing a passage of verse interpolation in the prose Merlin contests Gaster's view of the relative priority of the prose and poetical romances.

The Legend of Sir Perceval, 2 Vols. London, 1906, 1909; New York, 1972.

Vol. 1: Study of the Wauchier Continuation of Chrétien's *Conte del Graal*. Wauchier's source was older than Chrétien's; the Bleheris version of Gawain's adventure was earliest Grail story; the Grail was Christianized long before Chrétien wrote; in its non-Christian form the Grail is a food-producing talisman; in Bleheris the Grail-Gawain story is the confused remembrance of ancient Nature worship, the cult of Adonis or Tammuz. Behind romance lies folk-lore, behind folk-lore fragments of old religions. Vol. 2: Gives printed version of the Modena MS. of the prose *Perceval* (Didot-*Perceval*) and a reconstruction of lost verse Perceval romance of Robert de Borron; further elucidation of theory of ritual origins of Grail Mysteries in Celtic worship, particularly Welsh.

"Tristan Ménestrel – Extrait de la Continuation de *Perceval* par Gerbert, *R*, 35 (1906), 497–501.

The Tristan sections of Gerbert's Continuation are not original compositions or metrical versions of the prose *Tristan* as has been proposed, but remodelled early short episodic poems based upon earlier traditions recounted nowhere else. At the point the poem assumed present form, Gawain was still the leading knight, Lancelot played a sub-role, and Tristan's connection with Arthur was very slight, characteristics existing earlier than the prose version account. A French extract edited by Bédier is included.

"Legends of Wagner's Trilogy," in *The Volsunga Saga*. Ed. by Eirikr Magnusson. London, 1907.

The Wagnerian treatment of the Siegfried legend in *The Valkyrie*, *Siegfried*, and *Twilight of the Gods*, including commentary on changes in the legend made by Wagner for his versions.

Sir Gawain and the Lady of Lys. Vol. 7 in ARUM. London, 1907; New York, 1972.

Prose translation of Wauchier's account of the Castle Orguellous adventure and Gawain's visit to the Lady of Lys; essay and notes.

"The Grail and the Rites of Adonis," *F–L*, 18 (1907), 283–305.

Earliest Grail story has as its hero Gawain, not Perceval. Welsh Bleheris is the earliest author, not Chrétien, and in the story told by him (found in Wauchier's version) we must seek Grail origins. The source of the Grail story may be a survival, misunderstood, of a form of nature worship, specifically, the rites of Adonis as described by Frazer. Probably originally the Maimed King and Fisher King were distinct, one the god, the other the priest who presided at the ritual feast. At the inititation of the neophyte he would explain the wasteland, connecting it with the death or wounding of the central figure. Achievement of the quest restores the land or heals the king. The visit to the Grail Castle is an initiation manqué. The Grail story is only secondarily a quest; primarily, it is the romance of a failed opportunity. It is to redress the failure that the quest is undertaken.

Review of *The Heroic Saga-Cycle of Dietrich of Bern*, by F. E. Sandbach, *F–L*, 18 (1907), 118–19.

The writer shows how the monarch Theodoric, king of the Ostrogoths, became a hero of romance and assumed form by which he is known in the saga.

Review of *Thomas' Roman de Tristan*, ed. Joseph Bédier, *F–L*, 18 (1907), 231–34.

Tristan and Iseult story belongs to a stage earlier than and different from the courts of love. Bédier using several versions is able to reconstruct the romance as Thomas would have had it, then study sources. Not enough attention is given to Bréri (Bleheris) as a source. If Thomas drew from Bréri, then the originals must be episodic poems. Two traditions, each depicting a different kind of Mark, fed the story. Rejects Bédier's view of an English prose-*Tristan*.

Review of *The Irish Text Society*: "The Story of the Crop-Eared Dog," "The Story of the Eagle Boy," *F–L*, 20 (1909), 361–62.

That a genuine Irish Arthurian tradition actually existed would be of the highest importance to prove. These stories show nothing of the genuine tradition. The writer may have been familiar with literary aspects of the legend. Arthur and his knights are mere names here. Probably stories were redacted at a time when the legend was in final stage of development.

Review of *Ferguut*, ed. J. Verdan, *F–L*, 20 (1909), 114–15.

Of this new edition of a Dutch version of the Perceval story, the geographical location, Scotland, is noteworthy. At fault is editor's glaringly defective knowledge of the personages of Arthurian romance.

"A Hitherto Undiscovered Aspect of the Round Table," in *Mélanges offerts à Maurice Wilmotte*, Paris, 1910, 1–14.

Layamon's description of the Round Table as "turning" diverges from his ostensible source, Wace. A turning table would accommodate all guests within the hall by turning on a pivot so half the guests should always be within. There are many instances of turning castles, but not tables. A passage in Béroul's *Tristan* supports the turning ability of the Round Table. Layamon likely based his version on an insular version of Wace contining that tradition; Layamon and Béroul thus strengthen the argument for Celtic folk themes in Arthurian story. Turning can derive from solar myths.

"Alfred Nutt: An Appreciation," *F–L*, 21 (1910), 512–14.

This tribute to the Celticist notes his recognition of the evolutionary character of Arthurian romance, literary invention having played a secondary part, and his belief that folklore study might illuminate original elements, particularly Welsh and Irish, from which romance evolved. Before Nutt's plea for the insular, Celtic, and popular provenance of Arthurian tradition, the field was held by the "before Chrétien – chaos" group.

"The Quest of the Holy Grail," *Q*, 1 (1910), 524–35.

Answering A. E. Waite's review of her Perceval studies, she cites his concern for the Grail as primarily a Christian symbol while her interest is literature conveying the mystical or religious, such study as he belittles. Grail romances are records of actual experience of one who failed the test. This was remodelled along Christian lines and has reached us in a confused state. Waite dislikes folklore, thus refuses to accept the "debris of ritual" preserved in the folktale. His assertions are misleading.

"Arthurian Legend," "Guenevere," "The Holy Grail," "King Arthur," "Lancelot," "Sir Thomas Malory," "Walter Map," "Merlin," "Perceval," "The Round Table," "Tristan," "Wolfram von Eschenbach." *Encyclopaedia Britannica*. 11th Edition. London and New York, 1911; revised 1928.

Each is a full article with bibliography appended.

"The Caroles in Medieval Romance," *Q*, 2 (1911), 518–23.

There are three notable instances of the carol in Arthurian romance having "mystery" origin: (1) in the Vulgate Merlin, Merlin creates "caroles" for Viviane's diversion; (2) in *Meraugis de Portlesguez*, where a carol casts a spell over the hero; (3) in *Der Verlorenen Forest*, where Lancelot dances to a spell woven by King Ban. In all the stress is on dance, not song. "Caroles" were a survival of religious "mystery" dances and were later endowed with magical properties. Sacred character survived in the song as the dance died out.

"A Note on the Identification of the 'Bleheris' of Wauchier de Denain," *RC*, 32 (1911), 5–17.

Contains letter from Edward Owen supporting the claim of *The Legend of Sir Perceval* that Bleheris was important source of early Grail romances and was the Bledhericus referred to by Giraldus. Bledhericus is Latin form of Welsh Bledri, possibly Bledri ap Cadivor referred to in charters of 1129–1134 and author of some of Welsh "Chronicle of Princes." Cartulary confirmation uses term Bledhericus *Latemeri*, "latimarius" or interpreter, i.e., of romantic stories from Welsh to French.

Old English Carols From the Hill MS. London, 1911.

Carols from the sixteenth century Richard Hill Collection, Oxford, rendered into modern English.

Romance, Vision and Satire. Boston. 1912.

Translations of Middle English alliterative poems preserving original meters where possible, including *Sir Gawain and the Green Knight, The Adventure of Arthur at the Tarn Wadeling, Morte Arthure, Cleanness, Patience, Pearl, Piers Plowman* (parts of A and B); notes.

"The Madonna of Pontmain," *Q*, 4 (1913), 329–34.

Retells account by a priest at Church of St Roch, Paris, of an apparition of the Blessed Virgin he and five others witnessed in 1871 and urges further study of this manifestation.

The Quest of the Holy Grail. London, 1913; London, 1964.

The literature of the Grail cycles and a survey of leading theories, i.e., Christian, Celtic, ritual, concluding that the subject falls within field of comparative religion, particularly as Grail quest embodies elements of Adonis rites of ancient Mystery cults. Includes appendix on "The Grail Procession," with excerpts from Chrétien, Wolfram, the Didot-*Perceval*, the *Perlesvaus*, and *Diu Crône*.

"On the Independent Character of the Welsh *Owein*," *F–L*, 24 (1913), 254–56.

Continues her agreement with A. C. K. Brown that seeks to demolish Foerster's theory of dependence of Welsh Mabinogi "The Lady of the Fountain" on Chrétien's *Iwain*, but stresses points overlooked, particularly the folklore characters later adapted by Chrétien for sophisticated audience. The Welsh Mabinogi is a folk tale, not an other-world tale, and is independent of Chrétien.

The Chief Middle English Poets. Boston, 1914; New York, 1968.

Selections from principal branches of English medieval literature: history, legendaries, romance.

"Notes on the Grail Romances: *Sone de Nansai, Parzival* and *Perlesvaus*," *R*, 43 (1914), 403–26.

The 13th century *Sone de Nansai*, part of it set in Norway, offers version of the Grail legend different in essential points from other romances yet with parallels in other romances. Not an Arthurian poem or a Grail quest, yet this gives the history and whereabouts of the Grail. Gerbert may have used *Sone* in his Continuation; parallels throughout are with Perceval form of the quest.

There is connection between the *Perlesvaus* and the *Histoire de Fulk Fitz-Warin* in the "Blanche Lande Perilous Chapel" episode.

Germany's Crime Against France. London, 1915.

This pamphlet condemns the German slaughter of Belgian civilians and outrages against the French as barbarism and urges strengthened effort to defeat the invaders. Germany's aim has ever been the destruction of France and then of the British Empire. Unable to control France, Germany has determined to destroy her artistic and religious monuments in occupied provinces, has annihilated industry and agriculture. Savage mistreatment of civilian population must warn the English. The Germans say they are re-generating a decadent race and say the same of the English. She warns the professors beguiled by the great tradition of German scholarship that for Germany to remain unpunished would be an act against humanity.

"The Soul of France," *Q*, 6 (1915), 754–60.

Effects of the World War on France and horrors inflicted by Germany show the power of German militarism. Especially barbaric is the treatment of women and churches. Outrages have quickened French patriotism and relig-ious faith, both qualities deeply rooted in the French. This is a spiritual war to the French, the conflict one of faith against evil.

Germany's Literary Debt to France. London, 1915.

This reprint of an article in *The Quest* (q.v. below), attacks the German notion of cultural supremacy. Germany's literature is traceable to foreign models to unparalleled degree. Lesser poets and greater (Wolfram, Gott-fried) composed from French originals. In lyric poetry, the Minnesänger owed initial impulse to French chivalric tradition. The great poets are in the first ranks, but as followers not initiators. The German is not a spontaneous creator. Even if modern civilization owed her a debt, Germany has liquida-ted that debt in blood. German organization means obedience for ag-gression; its own masses have no inner rule of conduct. Germany poses most appalling danger civilization has ever faced. [Appeared originally in *Q*, 7 (1915), 228–38.]

"The Ruined Temple," *Q*, 8 (1916), 127–39.

A fictionalized reconstruction of an initiation into the Mysteries of the Grail described as a revelation of the source of life.

"Débout, les Morts!" *Q*, 9 (1918), 297–308.

A tale of the World War recounting a French legend of the appearance of a Knight Templar on Christmas Eve to summon the dead to battle in the Holy Land.

"Mystery Survivals in Mediaeval Romance," *Q*, 11 (1920), 228–38.

Announces forthcoming *From Ritual to Romance*, but here narrows to Mys-tery origin of Grail romance adventures popularly regarded as folk- or fairy-tale features. In the Fisher King, the Celtic School has suggested Finn's "Salmon of Wisdom," but source is the Messianic fish-meal and life-symbolism of the fish. Texts in the Old English Legendaries preserve allusions to "other-world" of the Mysteries, which may have belonged to Mystery tradition before it became Celtic folk- or fairy-tale.

"Notes on the Grail Romances: The *Perlesvaus* and the Prose *Lancelot*," *R*, 46 (1920), 314–29.

Strong objection is voiced here to theories of Ferdinand Lot. 1) Argues that the *Perlesvaus* represents original *Queste* section of the *Lancelot*, that there existed a stage in Lancelot story when Galahad was unknown and Lancelot was connected with Perceval. Objects to Lot's theory that single author wrote the *Lancelot* cycle. 2) Challenges Lot's idea that Lancelot's role in cycle originated with the author; just as the Tristan story grew by degrees, so did Lancelot's, displacing Gawain and Perceval. Intermediate stage is found in the *Perlesvaus* and there in its latest form.

From Ritual to Romance. London, 1920; New York, 1957.

"Final views" of the transformation of ritual of ancient Mystery religions of Tammuz-Adonis into the Grail quest of medieval romance with claim for Welsh provenance.

"The *Perlesvaus* and the *Vengeance Raguidel*," *R*, 47 (1921), 349–59.

These works used different sources of parallel stories; the same original was used by Wauchier. Thus, Wauchier's version agrees with main theme of *Vengeance Raguidel* but retains details of the *Perlesvaus*. There is no borrowing between these two romances; the *P* author followed Wauchier or Wauchier's source. Behind the *V.R.* and its derivatives lies the "Geste of Sir Gawain" group.

"Glastonbury and the Holy Grail," *F–L*, 32 (1921), 131–33.

Maintains that the *Perlesvaus*, the only romance that can be connected with Glastonbury, is more interested in the burial place of Arthur and Guenevere than in the home of the Grail. Identification of Corbenic with Glastonbury untenable. The Grail Castle is located near the sea, not near a lake or marsh, probably on the Welsh coast.

"Correspondence: 'The Legends of the Holy Grail'," *Q*, 13 (1922), 408–12.

Reply to an article disputing the *Conte del Graal* was first to join Celtic material with Grail-Perceval themes. 1) There was a composite poem used by Wauchier; the poem is also ultimate source of *Parzival*. Author of Wolfram's source and copyists of Chrétien's poem knew end of the story. 2) Grail significance was known by German writer as source of life. As vessel of initiation Grail is Cup, Dish, and the "holy" Grail – source of life wrought of no material substance. Two lines of fertility worship and fairy tale interweave in final stage of literary development to confusion of modern critics.

"Correspondence: 'A Shrieking Bog'," *F–L*, 34 (1923), 379–80.

Ulrich's *Lanzelet* contains section on castle situated on lake surrounded by a shrieking bog. At Solstice the bog shrieks from the heat of nearby stream. This local tradition may have been included in a book by Walter Map. Brought to Germany in 1194, the book may have been the original of the poem.

"The *Perlesvaus* and the Story of the Coward Knight," *MP*, 20 (1923), 379–89.

Here are compared stories of the Coward Knight in Manessier's Continuation and *P*. Nitze decided these are independent version of same original,

Manessier's the superior, but Weston contests this, holding to the *P* version as earlier and less confused. Concludes that 1) *P* author made independent use of material; 2) story derived from early stage of literature, fragments of which have survived in Wauchier and English Gawain poems.

"Notes on the Grail Romances: Caput Johannis=Corpus Christi," *R*, 49 (1923), 273–78.

Concerning reference to the head of John the Baptist as symbol of the Eucharist found in the York Breviary, the Caput Johannis=Corpus Christi identification (a local development in Yorkshire) may bear upon Grail appearance in *Peredur* where a bleeding head takes the place of Grail. This curious form may be the redactor's way of honoring "local cult" in Yorkshire, where there is a tradition of Peredur's burial place.

"The Evolution of Arthurian Romance," *BBCS*, 2 (1924), 173–84.

Points up Bruce's numerous inaccuracies as result of misreadings, incomplete transcripts or simple carelessness and defends her own theories. She acknowledges importance of Bruce's posthumous work; reminds readers of his narrow, conservative view of origins; holds that there *were* Arthurian romances before Chrétien and that the poet's exaggerated reputation has impeded progress of Arthurian criticism. She refutes Bruce's position on the existence of Mystery cults and his rejection of phallic symbolism of Lance-Grail; insists again on existence of poet Bleheris; attacks the Christian theory of the Grail as unsound.

"The Relation of the *Perlesvaus* to the Cyclic Romances," *R*, 51 (1925), 348–63.

Argues for an early 13th century date of *P* against view of Bruce and Lot of priority of the *Queste, Lancelot* and *Grand Saint Graal. GSG* represents the final stage of the cycle in which Galahad is the established Grail winner with hardly a hint of Perceval.

"Who Was Brian des Illes?" *MP*, 22 (1925), 405–11.

Brian de Insula, raised at the court of Henry II and probably well known, is the historical personage behind Brian des Illes in *P*. A romance in which he plays a part would have been composed while he was still in living memory. He is drawn unfavorably because of Norman domination of the Welsh.

"The Apple Tree Mystery in Arthurian Romance," *BJRL*, 9 (1925), 417–30.

This links an incident variously described in Wauchier's Continuation, the Didot-*Perceval*, and *Durmart le Galois* with the Mystery cults. Ultimate source of apple tree incident is *Le Pèlerinage de l'Ame*, an elaborate allegory on Adam, the apple, and a tree. The romances use imagery drawn from the drama, proving mutual dependence on a common source; also shows Christianization of pagan fertility of the orchard ritual, long known to folklorists as "wassailing the apple-trees," a ceremony lingering on in Britain as a folk custom. Mystery form remained as literary survival.

"The Relative Position of the *Perceval* and *Galahad* Romances," *MLR*, 21 (1926), 385–89.

Setting of *P* corresponds with conditions found in early 12th century where hermits rather than monks abound. In the Galahad *Queste* are few hermits, many monasteries, suggesting composition after reforms proposed by St Bernard had taken hold. Perceval story reflects older tradition, an evolving one traceable in the Continuations. Story took shape as Perceval-Grail quest in 12th century; Chrétien writing later recognized archaic character of material and tried to bring it up to date.

Review of *Celtic Myth and Arthurian Romance*, by Roger S. Loomis, *MLR*, 23 (1928), 243–48.

Loomis's object is to prove Arthurian themes originate in Old Irish god Curoi. Besides objecting to his derivation of names, she holds his method to be unsound as he insists that medieval writers were fully conscious of the original character of their material. She objects to his equating Perceval's sister with the Loathly Lady, to his interpretation of the Modena sculptures; she asserts the Grail ritual is mystical, its origins found in earlier ritual capable of Christianization – such as not to be found in Irish tradition. She rejects theory of Irish origins in favor of Welsh.

"Legendary Cycles of the Middle Ages," in *Cambridge Mediaeval History*. Vol. 6. Cambridge, 1928.

Extensive, comprehensive history of Arthurian and other cyclic literature of the Middle Ages; reprinted in recent editions.

The Romance of Perlesvaus. Ed. by Janet Grayson. Holland, Mich., 1988.

Study of major episodes showing retention of more primitive characteristics of "geste of Sir Gawain" group to prove there were Perceval romances before Chrétien, and that both the Didot-*Perceval* and the *P* (1191–1210) are older than the *Queste*.

APPENDIX II

The article following, "The Grail and the Rites of Adonis," appeared in the September 1907 number of *Folk-Lore*, the journal of the Folk-Lore Society of London. Weston read the paper, originally titled "The Grail and the Mysteries of Adonis," at a meeting of the Society in December, 1906. A lively discussion, with F. J. Furnivall, Alfred Nutt, A. B. Cook, and W. B. Yeats participating, followed the presentation. In 1906, also, Weston's first volume of *Perceval* studies appeared. In it she proposed that Gawain, not Perceval, was the original Grail hero, and set forth detailed preliminary theories of the Grail ceremonies as a re-enactment of a nature cult ritual. In "The Grail and the Rites of Adonis' she concluded that "the scene enacted in the presence of the chance visitor to the Grail Castle involved the chief incidents of the Adonis rites." The argument is continued and expanded in Volume II of *The Legend of Sir Perceval*, 1909. The article profits from simplicity as it presents the essentials of the ritual theory before the complications of Tarot cards, Attis-Mithra cults, and Gnostic doctrines were introduced. Several points Weston emphasized are worth noting: (1) the Grail quest as the consequence of the failure of the hero to ask the question; (2) the fusion of rich Grail or tailleor and Saint Sang legend; (3) the citing of Bleheris as the author of the original Gawain adventures in the *Perceval* Continuations; (4) the dual character of the Grail ritual and initiation into the secret meaning of the Grail. This particularly she insists upon. In "The Ruined Temple," published in *The Quest*, October 1916, we have a recreation of a successful initiation into the Grail Mysteries on two levels, the physical and spiritual sources of life. The emphasis is decidedly on the non-material, mystical Grail that unites the initiate to the god, an interpretation fully and finally developed in *From Ritual to Romance* in 1920. Weston accounts for features common to Grail ceremonies: the body on the bier, the Fisher King as the host, the Grail as food-producing talisman, the knight as initiate enduring a series of tests, and the Grail revealed in a splendid aureole of rosy light. The Grail temple stands on a headland looking out to sea, traditionally the site of Perceval's home and a site prominent in the *Perlesvaus*.

THE GRAIL AND THE RITES OF ADONIS

In offering these remarks on the subject of the Grail origins, I should wish to be understood as seeking, rather than tendering, information. The result of my researches into the *Perceval* legend has been to cause me to form certain opinions as to the sources of the Grail story, which the exigencies of space, and the character of the *Studies* as a whole, prevented me from setting forth fully in the published volume. At the same time these conclusions bore so directly on folklore researches that I was strongly impressed with the desirability of bringing them to the attention of trained folklorists, that I might have the advantage of their criticism and judgment in finally formulating my theory. Not that I can claim to be the first to give expression to such views. Long since Simrock, in his translation of the *Parzival*, and Professor Martin, in his *Zur Gralsage Untersuchungen* (1880), arrived at very similar conclusions, but at that time the critical material at their disposal was scanty. We lacked the illuminating labours of Mannhardt and his disciple, Dr J. G. Frazer. We had but one *Perceval* text, and that an extremely bad one, at our disposal, and in consequence the results obtained, though interesting and stimulating, were hardly convincing.

Hitherto, in criticising the Grail legend, we have been under the grave disadvantage of uncertainty as to the relative position of the extant versions of the story; we were not sure which of the varying forms represented most faithfully the original *données* of the tale. It is obvious that this was a serious hindrance. You cannot safely theorize as to the original form of a story while you are still in doubt as to which of certain widely differing versions is the older. Inasmuch as, in point of MS date, the *Perceval* of Chrétien de Troyes is the oldest of our Grail romances, the tendency has been to regard the story as told by him as the most nearly approaching the original, and to argue from that; although the vague and unsatisfactory details there given left it open to conjecture whether the author were dealing with a tradition already formed, or with one in process of formation.

Now, owing to recent discoveries, the standpoint has been shifted back, and we know that the earliest attainable Grail story is that of which not Perceval but Gawain was the hero, and the authorship of which is ascribed not to Chrétien de Troyes, but to Bleheris the Welshman. The date at which Bleheris lived is uncertain, but his identity alike with the Bledhericus referred to by Giraldus Cambrensis, and the Bréri quoted as authority for the *Tristan* of Thomas, has been frankly accepted by the leading French and American scholars; so far the Germans have preserved silence on the subject.

The passage in Giraldus is unfortunately very vague; he simply refers to Bledhericus as '*famosus ille fabulator*,' and says he lived 'a little before our time,' words which may mean anything. Giraldus may be using the editorial 'we,' and may mean 'a little before my time,' which, as he was writing in the latter half of the twelfth century, might imply that Bledhericus lived in the earlier half. But he may also have used the pronoun quite indefinitely; as M. Ferdinand Lot, with whom I discussed the question, remarked, "it may mean anything from ten to a hundred years; we might say that Bonaparte lived 'a little before our time'." When we take into consideration the fact that only three distinct references to Bleheris, or Blihis, as a source, have been preserved, while the name is more frequently found in the duplicated form of Bleo-Bleheris, Blihos-Blihéris, or Bliobliheri, and generally attached to a knight of Arthur's court, it seems most probable that he lived at a period sufficiently remote to allow of the precise details concerning his life and work to become obscured, while the tradition of his close connection with Arthurian romance was retained. In any case this much is certain, and this is what principally concerns us, his version of the Grail story is older than that of Chrétien, and we are justified in seeking for indications of origin in the story as told by him rather than in the version of the younger poet.

This is the Bleheris Grail story, as given by Wauchier de Denain, in his continuation of the *Perceval*.

Arthur, at the conclusion of his successful expedition against Chastel Orguellous, has given the queen *rendez-vous* at certain cross roads, marked by four pine trees. Here the court awaits him. One evening the queen is playing chess at the entrance of her pavilion when a stranger knight rides past, and fails to offer any salutation. Indignant at the apparent discourtesy, the queen sends Kay after him to command his return. Kay, as is his wont, carries out his commission in so ungracious and insulting a manner that he is overthrown for his pains, and returns to court with an exaggerated account of the knight's bearing and language. Gawain is then dispatched on the same errand, and, overtaking the stranger, courteously invites his return, but is told that he rides on a quest that will brook no delay, and which none but he may achieve; nevertheless, he thinks it possible that Gawain, whose identity he has learned, might succeed. On his return he will gladly pay his respects to the queen.

Gawain, however, by soft words, persuades him to return, pledging his honour that he shall in no wise suffer by the delay. They turn back, but scarcely have they reached the tents when the knight with a loud cry, falls forward, wounded to death by a javelin cast by an unseen hand. With his dying breath he bids Gawain don his armour, and mount his steed, which shall carry him to the destined goal. Gawain, furious at the slur cast on his honour by this breach of his safe-conduct, does as requested, and, leaving the dead body to the care of the queen, departs at once.

Through the night he rides, and all the next day, till he has passed the borders of Arthur's land, and at nightfall, wearied out, he finds himself in a waste land by the sea-shore. A causeway, bordered on either side by trees, their roots in the water, runs out from the land, and at the further end Gawain sees a light, as of a fire. The road is so dark and the night so stormy, he would fain delay till morning, but the steed, taking the bit in its teeth, dashes down the pathway, and eventually he reaches the entrance to a lighted hall. Here he is at first received as one long-expected, but, having unhelmed, is seen to be a stranger, and left alone. In the centre of the hall stands a bier, on which lies a body, covered with a rich pall of crimson silk, a broken sword on the breast, and four censers at the four corners of the bier. A procession of clergy enters, headed by a silver cross, and followed by many folk. Vespers for the dead are sung amid general lamentation, and Gawain is again left alone. He now sees on the dais a Lance, fixed in a silver socket, from which a stream of blood flows continuously in to a golden cup, and thence, by a channel, is carried out of the hall. Servants prepare the tables for a meal, and the King of the castle, entering, greets Gawain kindly, and seats him beside him on the dais. The butlers pour wine into the cups, and from a doorway there issues '*The rich Grail*,' which serves them; otherwise there is '*nor serjant nor seneschal*,' and Gawain marvels much at the service of the Grail, for now 'tis here, and now there, and for fear and wonder he scarce dare eat. After supper the King leads Gawain to the bier, and, handing him the broken sword, bids him resolder it. This he fails to do, and the King, shaking his head, tells him he may not accomplish the quest on which he has come; nevertheless, he has shewn great valour in coming thither, and he may ask what he will; he shall be answered. Gawain asks of the Lance: 'tis the Lance of Longinus, with it the side of the Saviour was pierced, as he hung on the Cross, and it shall remain where it now is, and bleed, till the Day of Doom. The King will tell who it is who lies on the bier, of the stroke by which he met his death, and the destruction brought on the land thereby, but as he speaks, weeping the while, Gawain falls asleep, and wakes to find himself upon the seashore, his steed fastened to a rock beside him, and all trace of the castle vanished. Wondering much, he mounts his steed, and rides through a land no longer waste, while all the folk he meets bless and curse him; for, by asking concerning the Lance, he has brought about the partial restoration of fruitfulness. Had he also asked of the Grail, the curse would have been entirely removed.

Now, there are certain points in this story which cannot fail to strike those familiar with the Grail legend. Who are the two dead men of the tale, the knight so mysteriously slain and the Body on the bier? We never learn. Nor do we ever hear the nature of the quest – Was it to avenge the dead knight of the castle? Was it to break the spell upon the land? Manessier, who about fifty years later brought the *Perceval* compilation to a final conclusion, gives, indeed, what purports to be a continuation of the tale. Gawain is here besought by the sister of the knight slain in his company to come to her aid against a foe, but the story is *banale* to the last degree. There are points of contact with other versions: the maiden's name is '*la sore pucele*,' the name Chrétien gives to the Grail King's niece; her foe is King Mangons, or Amangons, the name of the oppressor of the maidens in the *Elucidation*, to which we shall refer presently; but if there be any original connection with the Bleheris version, that connection has become completely obscured. Manessier, too, makes no attempt at solving the mystery of the Body upon the bier: certain scholars have indeed identified the slain man with Goon-Desert, or Gondefer, the brother of Manessier's Grail King, whose death by treachery Perceval avenges. But this identification is purely arbitrary; there is no bier in Manessier; it is, in fact, distinctively a feature of the *Gawain* version.

The connection of the wasting of the land with the death of the knight, if knight he were, is also uncertain; indeed this is a part of the story which appears to have been designedly left in obscurity – it is at this point that Gawain falls asleep. I am tempted to believe that those who told the tale were themselves at a loss here. Then the Grail is no Christian relic, it acts simply as a food-providing talisman, coming and going without visible agency. It is called the *rich*, not the *holy*, Grail. Nor does the explanation given of the Lance agree with the description; the stream of blood, which pours continuously from the weapon, and is carried out of the hall, whither, we are not told, can have no connection with the carefully-guarded relic of the *Saint Sang*. In truth, we may say without any hesitation that the whole machinery of the story is definitely non-Christian, and that the explanation of its peculiarities must be sought outside the range of ecclesiastical tradition. At the same time certain of these features are repeated in persistent fashion, even in the most definitely ecclesiasticised versions; a peculiarity which, I think, justifies, the supposition that they form a part of the original Grail tradition.

Now it has seemed to me that an explanation of the most characteristic features of our story may be found in the suggestion that they are a survival, misunderstood and imperfectly remembered, of a form of Nature worship closely allied to, if not identical with, the Rites of Adonis so exhaustively studied by Dr Frazer in *The Golden Bough*. It will be remembered that the essence of these rites was the symbolic representation of the annual processes of Nature, the sequence and transition of the seasons. The god, Adonis, or Tammuz, or whatever he was called in the land where the rites were celebrated, typified the vivifying principle of vegetation; his death was mourned as the death of vegetation in winter, his restoration to life was hailed as its restoration in spring. An effigy representing the dead god was honoured with all the rites of mourning, and subsequently committed to the waves. Women especially played so large a part in these rites that an Arabic writer of the tenth century refers to the festival as El-Bugât, '*the festival of the Weeping Women.*'

The central *motif* of the Gawain Grail-story is, I submit, identical with the central idea of the Adonis rites – a death, and failure of vegetation caused by that death. Both here and in the version given by the curious German poem of *Diû Crône*, where Gawain is again the Grail hero, we are told that the wasting of the land was brought about by the *Dolorous Stroke*. Thus the central figure, the Body on the bier, whose identity is never made clear, would in this view represent the dead god; the bleeding Lance, the weapon with which he was done to death (I think it more probable that the *Dolorous Stroke* was dealt by a Lance or Spear, as in the *Balin and Balan* story, than by a sword).

If we accept this view we can, I think, explain the origin of that mysterious figure of the Grail legend, the Maimed King. The fact that this central figure was at the same time dead and alive must, when the real meaning of the incidents had become obscured, and the story, imperfectly remembered, was told simply as a story, have been a source of perplexity to the tellers. An easy way out of the difficulty – it was a very real difficulty – would be to represent the king, or god, as desperately wounded. That such an idea was in the minds of the romance writers appears, I think, from the peculiar version of *Diû Crône*, where, when Gawain has asked concerning the Grail, the Maimed King and his attendants vanish at daybreak; they were dead, but preserved a semblance of life till the question was put. If the *Gawain* versions really represent the older, and

66

primary, group, it is possible that this particular rendering really preceded the Maimed King version, though in the form preserved it is combined with it.

Again, in the very curious and unique *Merlin* MS, No. 337 of the French MSS of the *Bibliothèque Nationale*, we find that Perceval is called the son of the widow lady, while his father, the Maimed King, is yet alive, and it is explained that, being desperately wounded, and only to be healed when the quest is achieved, he is as good as dead, and his wife may be reckoned a widow. These two instances will suffice to show that the transformation of the Body on the bier into the Maimed King on the litter, is neither impossible nor unnatural. The two are really one and the same.

Students of the Grail cycle will hardly need to be reminded that the identity of the Maimed King is a hopeless puzzle. He may be the Fisher King, or the Fisher King's father, or have no connection with either, as in the Evalach-Mordrains story. He may have been wounded in battle, or accidentally, or wilfully, or by supernatural means, as the punishment of too close an approach to spiritual mysteries. A proof of this confusion which ultimately resulted from these conflicting versions is to be found in the *Merlin* MS above referred to, where not only Perceval's father but two others are Maimed Kings, and all three sit at the Table of the Grail. If such confusion existed in the mind of the writers, no wonder that we, the readers, find the path of Grail criticism a rough and intricate one! Probably the character of the Maimed King and the Fisher King were originally distinct, the Maimed King representing, as we have suggested, the god, in whose honour the rites were performed; the Fisher King, who, whether maimed or not, invariably acts as host, representing the Priest. It would be his office to preside at the ritual feast, and at the initiation of the neophyte, offices which would well fit in with the character of Host. Here, the name of Fisher King is not given to him, but in certain texts which interpolate the history of Joseph of Arimathea he is identified with that Monarch. It will readily be understood that when the idea that the god was alive gained possession of the minds of those who told the story, there would be two lords of the castle, and they would find some difficulty in distinguishing the role of the one from that of the other. We may note that in this (i.e., the Bleheris) version, in that of Wauchier de Denain at the conclusion of his section of the *Perceval*, in the Prose *Lancelot*, and in the *Queste*, the Host is not maimed.

Again, this proposed origin would explain the wasting of the land, the mysterious Curse of Logres, which is referred to alike in earlier and later versions, and of which no explanation is ever given. As we saw above, the essence of the Rites was the symbolic representation of the processes of Nature. The festival of the death and revival of the god took place at the Spring solstice; it was an objective parable, finding its interpretation in the awakening of Nature from her winter sleep. Here the wasting of the land is in some mysterious manner connected with the death or wounding of the central figure; the successful accomplishment of the Grail quest brings about either the restoration of the land to fruitfulness, or the healing of the King (Chrétien and Wolfram, for example, have no Waste Land). Thus the object of the Quest would appear to be one with that of the Adonis-ritual.

This wasting of the land is found in three *Gawain* Grail-stories, that by Bleheris, the version of *Chastel Merveilleus*, and *Diu Crône*; it is found in one *Perceval* text, the Gerbert continuation. Thus, briefly, the object of the Rites is the restoration of Vegetation, connected with the revival of the god; the object of the Quest is the same, but connected with the restoration to health of the King.

I have before noted the fact that the role played by women in these rites was of such importance that eventually it gave a name to the Festival. In the Notes to my translation of three visits paid by Gawain to the Grail Castle, I remarked on the persistent recurrence in these stories of a weeping maiden or maidens, the cause of whose grief is never made clear. In *Diu Crône*, where, as we have seen, the Maimed King and his court have but the semblance of life and are in very truth dead, the Grail-bearer and her companions are the only living beings in the castle, and their grief is, in a measure, comprehensible; they desire the breaking of the spell which binds them to this uncanny company. In what, in the *Perceval Studies*, I have designated as the *Chastel Merveilleus* version, a version midway between that of Bleheris and of Chrétien, there is but one weeping maiden, the Grail-bearer. In the curious interpolation of the Heralds' College MS, when the broken sword is restored to the Fisher King, he mentions among the results of the successful achievement of the quest, that the hero shall know why the maiden weeps. I doubt very much whether the writer of the lines himself knew the reason! In the visit paid by Bohort to Castle Corbenic, it is Elaine, daughter of King Pelles, who weeps, because, being no longer a maiden, she may no longer be Grail-bearer. As she is about to become the mother of the Grail-winner, and knows to what honour her son is predestined, the explanation is not convincing; but there had to be a weeping maiden in the story. The most curious instance of the persistence of this part of the original tradition is to be found in Gawain's visit to Corbenic, in the prose *Lancelot*, where he sees not one, but twelve maidens kneeling at the closed door of the Grail chamber, weeping bitterly, and praying to be delivered from their torment. But the dwellers in Castle Corbenic, so far from being in torment, have all that heart can desire, and, moreover, the honour of being guardians of the (here) sacred and most Christian relic, the Holy Grail.

Now, in the light of the parallels already cited, is it not at least possible that these weeping maidens, who wail so mysteriously through the Grail story, are a survival of, and witness to, the original source of that story, that they are the mourning women of the Adonis ritual, the 'Women weeping for Tammuz'?

This interpretation would also explain the constant stress laid upon the *general* mourning, even when the reason for this mourning appears inadequate, as e.g. in the *Parzival*. Here we are told that the appearance of the bleeding Lance is the signal for such lamentation that *"The folk of thirty kingdoms could scarce have bemoaned them more,"* Bk. v, 1. 130. Here certainly the Lance is that with which the king has been wounded, but the *folk* of the castle are in no way affected, there is no wasting of the land.

Again, in *Peredur*, at the appearance of the lance all fell to wailing and lamentation, but here there seems to be no connection between the Lance and the wound of the king, which latter is the work of the sorceresses of Gloucester.

If the original source of the story is to be found in the Adonis ritual, and if the mourning which is so marked a feature of that ritual be associated, as Drs Robertson Smyth and Farnell have suggested, rather with the death of the god than with the consequent failure of vegetation, when we might expect to find the association of the mourning with the weapon which originally dealt the fatal blow to persist in versions which had dropped out the (originally) companion feature of the Wasted Land.

We have thus the following important points of contact between the Adonis ritual and the story of the Visit to the Grail Castle: the wasted land; the slain king (or knight); the mourning, with special insistence on the part played by women; and the restoration of fertility; while certain minor points, such as the crimson covering of the bier, the incense, and the presence, in certain versions, of doves as agents in the mysterious ceremonies also find their parallel in the same ritual.

To put the matter briefly, the scene enacted in the presence of the chance visitor to the Grail Castle involved the chief incidents of the Adonis rites. I would submit that whereas the presence of an isolated feature might be due to chance, that of a complete and harmonious group, embracing at once the ceremonies and the object of the cult, can scarcely be so explained.

To go a step further. Originally I entitled this paper *The Grail and the Mysteries of Adonis*. For the word *mysteries* I have now substituted *ritual*, in view of the perfectly well-grounded objection that, in classical times, the worship of Adonis was not carried on in secret. Nevertheless, I am disposed to believe that the word *mysteries* might, without impropriety, be used in connection with the celebration of these rites when in later ages Christianity had become the faith 'in possession,' and the votaries of an older cult performed their rites under the ban of ecclesiastical disapproval. Much, of course, depends upon the character of the cult; the Adonis worship was in its essence a 'Life' cult, the life of the god ensuring the life of vegetation, and that in its turn the life of man; it is obvious that such a cult might possess an esoteric as well as an exoteric significance. To the ordinary worshipper the ritual would be an object-lesson, setting forth the actual processes of Nature, to the initiate it would be the means of imparting other, and less innocent, teaching as to the sources of life.

This much is certain: the Grail is perpetually treated as something strange, mysterious, awe-inspiring; its secrets are on no account to be rashly approached or lightly spoken of; he runs great danger who dares so. Such terms could hardly be applied to the Adonis rites under ordinary conditions, and yet, as we have seen, the Grail story presents such a striking identity of incident with these rites that a connection between the two seems practically certain. We have to seek for some explanation which will preserve this connection while at the same time accounting for the presence of certain 'occult' features in the tale.

The explanation surely lies in the fact suggested above, that the Adonis cult was essentially a Life cult, and, as such, susceptible of strange developments. Dr Frazer has laid stress on the close connection which, in the minds of primitive worshippers, subsisted between the varying forms of life: "They commonly believed that the tie between the animal and vegetable world was even closer than it really is – to them the principle of life and fertility, whether animal or vegetable, was one and indivisible." Dulaure, while assigning the same *origin* as does Dr Frazer to the ritual, definitely classes the worship of Adonis among those cults which "assumed in process of time a distinctly 'carnal' character."

The Lance and Cup which form the central features of the imagery of our story are also met with as 'Phallic' symbols, and I am strongly of opinion that many of the most perplexing features of the legend are capable of explanation on the theory that behind the ordinary simple 'Vegetation' symbolism there lay something which justified so learned and acute a scholar as the late Professor Heinzel, whose works are a veritable mine of learning and ingenuity, in regarding our records of the Visit to the Grail Castle as records of an initiation *manqué*. Long since, in his study on the Old French Grail romances (*Die Alt-Französische Gral Romanen*, 1891) he suggested that the failure to put the question was equivalent to a refusal on the part of the neophyte to submit to the ordeal, but, owing probably to the form in which he cast the results of his researches, much of their value has been obscured.

Let us note first, that whatever else changes in the story, the essential framework remains the same. Always the castle is found by chance; always the hero beholds marvels he does not comprehend; always he fails to fulfil the test which would have qualified him to receive the explanation of those marvels; always he recognises his fault too late, when the opportunity has passed beyond recall; and only after long trial is it again granted to him. Let us clear our minds once and for all from the delusion that the Grail story is *primarily* the story of a quest; it is that *secondarily*. In its primary form it is the romance of a lost opportunity; for always, and in every instance, the first visit connotes failure; it is to redress that failure that the quest is undertaken. So essentially is this a part of the story that it survives even in the Galahad version; that immaculate and uninteresting hero does not fail, of course; but neither does he come to the Grail castle for the first time when he presides at the solemn and symbolic feast; he was brought up there, but has left it before the Quest begins; like his predecessors, Gawain and Perceval, he goes forth from the castle in order to return.

Now, let us accept for the nonce Professor Heinzel's suggestion, but for the word *refusal* substitute *failure*, and recognising that the incidents related rest upon real objective facts, we may, perhaps, hazard a guess at the cause of this failure. In the Bleheris story we have seen that the hero was overcome by slumber at the critical moment of the King's recital, and only awoke to find himself alone upon the seashore, all trace of the castle having disappeared. This is again the cause of failure in the *Chastel Merveilleus* version. In the *Perlesvaus* three drops of blood fall from the lance on to the table, and Gawain, gazing upon them, falls into a trance, and can neither speak nor stir. In *Diû Crône* we have again the mysterious slumber, though here associated with the drinking of wine, the effect of which is to plunge Gawain's comrades, Lancelot and Calogreant, into a sleep which lasts till the question has been put, and the marvels explained. In this version also, we have the blood drops; but here, though they fall from the Lance, they are swallowed by the King, thus having no connection with the trance.

In the *Perceval* version, on the contrary, the blood drops are connected with a trance, but not with the Grail; and the hero's failure is accounted for on purely rational grounds, his too rigid adherence to the counsels of Gurnemanz.

As we have seen, the *Gawain* versions certainly represent the older stage of tradition, and we may, therefore, fairly assume that, in the original form of the story, the failure to ask the necessary question was due to a mysterious slumber which overtook the hero at the crucial point of his test. But what caused this slumber? Is it too bold a suggestion that the blood drops, which are often so closely associated with the Grail, and are always found in connection with a trance, were the operating cause? that, in fact, they were employed to induce an hypnotic slumber on the part of the aspirant? We know that in Mesmerism and kindred practices, the first step is to seize and fix the attention of the subject – I believe a glittering disc, or some such object, is often employed – in any case it is through the eye that the desired effect is produced upon the brain. In the case of Gawain, and of Perceval alike, we are told that it is the startling contrast of colour – the crimson blood on the white cloth, or snow – that fetters their attention. It is of course *possible* that the slumber was merely a literary device for winding up the story, but the introduction of the feature of restored vegetation shows that the tale was moulded by someone who understood its real significance; and slumber hypnotically induced would be a very natural method of getting rid of an intruder who had stumbled upon rites not intended for general knowledge, and had failed to qualify for admission to their secrets. This much is certain if the Grail stories have their root in the ritual of Adonis, we are dealing with a set of concrete facts, which must originally have admitted of a rational explanation. I would submit that if the slumber be really a part of the original tale, and there is every reason to believe that it is, then it must be capable of a rational explanation, and I can, in no other way, account for its constant recurrence, or for its connection with the blood drops, save on the hypothesis that one of the trials to which the neophyte was exposed, and to which apparently he frequently succumbed, was the test of hypnotic suggestion.

But how shall we explain the Grail itself? Would it not be the vessel of the common quasi-sacramental feast always connected with these rites? It is interesting that the MS which gives us the best Bleheris text also, in the same section of the work, offers us the only other instance I know of the use of the word Grail. When Gawain enters the castle of Brandelis, he finds a feast prepared, and boars' heads upon Grails of silver. The other MSS have here substituted for *Grail* the word *Tailléor*. It is thus practically certain that the writer of these tales, when he used the word *Grail*, meant a Dish, and not a Cup. The magical features, the automatic service, the feeding of the guests with all kinds of meat, were probably later additions, borrowed by the story-tellers from the numerous food-providing talismans of folk lore. For we must ask ourselves how was the story told, from the inside or from the outside? That is, was it intended to be a method of preserving, and handing on, the tradition of these rites; or was it simply a story composed round this ritual as a centre? The first hypothesis would appear to involve the admission that the minstrels were the *conscious* guardians and transmitters of an occult tradition; a view which, in face of the close connection now proved to exist between the minstrel guilds and the monasteries, I do not feel able to accept. Also, we should then expect to find one clear and consistent version; and I suspect that that version would have been less susceptible of Christianisation. But if the tale were told from the outside, if it were a story based upon, quite possibly, the genuine experience of one who assisted by chance at the celebration of these rites, ignorant of their nature and meaning, we can understand how it would take and keep this particular form. One admitted to the full participation in this ritual might not talk about it, where one possessed of but a partial and outside knowledge would be free to speak. And as the story passed from one to the other, is it not probable that while the initiated might venture to add or correct a feature, the uninitiated would introduce details which appeared to him suitable, but which were really foreign to the original trend of the tale? How, except on the hypothesis of some such origin, explain the persistent adherence to the framework of the story, or the hunts as to the mysterious nature of the talisman, and the penalties to be incurred if its secrets are revealed? Do not let us forget that it is precisely in this, the earliest form of the tale, and in the confused version of the same offered by the *Elucidation*, that the *secret* character of the Grail is insisted upon. On any other hypothesis, what is this secret?

And now that I have had occasion to mention the *Elucidation*, I would ask, does not this theory of the Grail origins provide us, at last, with a possible solution of that most perplexing text? As is known to students of the subject, the *Elucidation* purports to be an introduction to the Grail story, and is found in three texts, the Mons MS of the *Perceval*, the Middle German translation of the continuation to that poem, and the (1530) printed edition of the work. It is extremely confused, and its connection with the other Grail texts has till recently been a complete puzzle. It starts with a warning from Master Blihis against revealing the secrets of the Grail. It then relates how at one time there were maidens dwelling in the hills, or wells, (the original word, *puys*, might be translated either way; I prefer the rendering of the German text, hills), who would offer food and drink to the passer by; but when King Amangons offered force to one, and took away her golden cup, they left the country; and, the writer goes on, "the court of the Fisher King could no longer be found." Nevertheless, Gawain found it; and we then have a summary of the Bleheris visit, given in terms often verbally identical with the text of Wauchier de Denain.

Some time ago, in the course of my *Perceval* studies, I came to the conclusion that the text at the root of the *Elucidation* was another, and apparently later, form of that used by Wauchier, and that in our English *Gawain* poems we had fragments of the same collection. Now, it appears to me, we can suggest even a closer link. What if this text be really what it purports to be, the introduction to all the Grail stories? If it be the record of an insult offered by a local chieftain to a priestess or these rites, in consequence of which they were no longer openly celebrated in that land, and, as the writer puts it, "the court of the Fisher King (the Priest of this ritual) could no longer be found," would not that be the logical introduction to the tale of one who found, and knew not what he found? It may be that after all the *Elucidation* is not so badly named!

So far as the Christian aspect of the story is concerned, it is now beyond doubt that a legend, similar in all respects to that of the Grail, was widely current at a date long anterior to any of our extant Grail texts. The story, with Nicodemus instead of Joseph as protagonist, is told of two of the most famous of Continental relics, the *Saint Sang* of Fescamp and the *Volto Santo* of Lucca. The most complete MSS of the *Perceval* refer, as authority, to a book written at Fescamp. Who was the first to utilise the pseudo-Gospels as material for the history of mediaeval relics we cannot say, but, given the trend of popular thought, it was practically inevitable that if the Grail were to receive the Christian pedigree which in the natural process of development in a mediaeval atmosphere, given to edification, it was bound to receive, it was almost inevitable that it should be fathered upon either Joseph of Arimathea or Nicodemus; as a matter of fact both are called into the service of the romancers.

Given these facts, on the one hand an exceedingly popular story, having for its central point of interest a vessel round which there hovered an atmosphere of mystery and dream – none dare speak of the secrets of the Grail – and connected in some unexplained manner with drops of blood and a bleeding lance: on the other hand, an equally popular legend connected with the Passion of Christ, and relics of that Passion; and does it not become easy to understand how on the common ground of the vessel of the ritual feast the two might meet, and eventually coalesce; the vessel of the Nature-worship being first connected with the Passion and finally identified with the chalice of the Eucharist. If I be correct in my suggestion as to the hidden meaning of this ritual, and that it was in truth a Life-cult, the Grail quest would be the quest for life; the Grail itself, under all its varying forms, the vessel in which the food necessary for life was presented to the worshippers.

I would earnestly ask all students of this fascinating subject to consider seriously whether the theory here sketched may not be found capable of providing that link between the conflicting versions which all previous hypotheses have failed to supply? On the theory of a purely Christian origin, how can we account for the obviously folk lore features of our tale? How could the vessel of the Christian Eucharist have become the self-acting, food-providing talisman, known not only to Bleheris, but also to the author of the *Queste*? How could Kiot, (the author of the lost French poem adapted by Wolfram von Eschenbach), have dared to turn it into a mere magical stone, a Baetylus? For if there be one thing certain, it is that the Grail had been Christianised before the day of Chrétien and Kiot. If, on the other hand, the vessel were a mere food-providing Pagan talisman, how, and why, did it become so suddenly Christianised? What was there about it, more than about the countless similar talismans, that would suggest such a development? But if the Grail were from the first connected with a form of religious worship, from the first surrounded with a halo of awe and reverence, we can understand that it would lend itself with admirable readiness to the process of Christianisation. Even as we can understand how Kiot, who was certainly a man of unusual learning, while he might shrink from Paganising a fundamentally Christian relic, would have no scruple in substituting the object of one mysterious Pagan cult for that of another, and in replacing the vessel of the Adonis Rites by a Baetylus. One who knew so much may well have known what was the real character of the Grail. It seems to me that on this theory, and on this theory alone, can we account logically and harmoniously, alike for the development and the diversities of the Grail romances.

It is scarcely necessary to remind members of this Society that, in the interesting series of papers on the European Sky-God, contributed by Mr Cook to the pages of *Folk-Lore*, certain stories connected alike with Cuchullin and Gawain, are claimed as dependent on, and to be explained by, precisely the set of customs and beliefs with which I am dealing here. If the Green Knight be a survival of the Vegetation god, why not the Maimed King? I do not know how far Mr Cook's theories have met with the approval of folk-lore experts, but it does seem to me that when two enquirers, starting from different points, and travelling by different roads, reach precisely the same goal, there is at least an initial probability that that goal was once, very long ago, no doubt, the starting point of those diverging roads.

THE RUINED TEMPLE

The traveller looked around him. He was standing on a headland jutting out into the sea. The summit of the cliff as far inland as eye could reach was a wild moorland studded with clumps of gorse and heather, now, in the middle of August, a glory of gold and purple.

At intervals amidst the low clumps of heather stood blocks of grey stone and fallen masonry, scattered, irregular in outline. Yet it was not difficult for a trained eye to discern a certain order and design in their relative positions. Evidently they explained themselves to the observer, for he nodded with keen satisfaction as his eye followed their outline.

"Yes, the building must have been here on the brow of the cliff looking seaward. These blocks give the outline approximately – circular evidently. And those monoliths further back mark the approach. Now what was it? – castle – temple?"

His eye fell upon a mound higher, of larger extent, than the surrounding clumps of heather and gorse. It was overgrown with brambles and tall bracken, and the outline was but ill-defined; still there was that about it which betrayed a not altogether fortuitous origin.

He strolled up to it, and began to probe about with his stout walking-stick. The soil was shallow. At the depth of perhaps a foot the stick struck on something hard and unyielding.

"Thought as much," he muttered to himself. "There was something here." He walked round, still probing carefully with his stick as he did so. In the midst of the tangle he met with no impenetrable resistance, but at either end, for perhaps a couple of feet, there was evidently stone or masonry. He drove his stick upward through the tangle of growth. At about three feet from the ground he again met a similar obstacle, this time for the depth of a few inches only.

Carefully following this he found that the upper stonework continued at either end somewhat beyond the lower.

"A block of stone on supports of stone or masonry obviously. Now was it a table or an altar?"

He looked round him keenly. The erection, be it what it might, was placed midway between the heather-encircled blocks of stone. Facing seaward he saw straight in front of him, rising from the tangle of gorse and heather, two corresponding monoliths some six feet in height; one still stood erect, the other had sunk sideways to an acute angle. In their original positions they would have framed, for one standing where he stood, a full view of the western sky. At this moment the sun within half an hour of setting was shining full in his face.

He wheeled round. Directly behind him were again monoliths apparently corresponding in height and relative position to the western pair. He paced the distance from the mound to each group. It was practically the same allowing for the irregularities of the over-growth. He uttered an exclamation of satisfaction.

"Temple evidently! This was the altar; and there were openings east and west for the rising and setting sun. Probably there was one in the roof directly above the altar for the midday. An ordinary dwelling would hardly be so planned. Now who were the people who used it?"

Seating himself on the ground, his back to the altar mound, facing the western outlook, he opened his knapsack and proceeded to make his evening meal of sandwiches and hard-boiled eggs washed down by a bottle of cider. Then lighting his pipe he lay down, hat over his eyes, and proceeded to muse drowsily over his problems.

Who and what had been the people who worshipped in this ruined sanctuary?

The Druids? In that case he would have expected to find trees near at hand. Certainly we knew but little of the details of Druidic worship. Yet if we bore in mind the important part the oak played in their ritual, would they have been likely to build a temple in so bare and sparsely wooded a district? He had seen no tree worthy the name in his day's tramp.

If not the Druids, who then? The early Celtic dwellers in these islands? "We know precious little of their beliefs and practices," he muttered to himself. Had there been any other folk? Any settlement? This was a coast-line. Suddenly a thought struck him and he sat up. "By Jove! yes, the Phoenicians!" It was not unlikely. This part of the country had once been rich in tin mines. They had fallen out of working long since; but the tradition remained. And his keen eye had noted in certain of the village churches he had explored quaint symbols which he knew to be derived from the old-time community of miners. Clasping his hands round his knees he looked steadily westward. Yes, there might have been a Phoenician colony here in long-forgotten days. They might have built this temple and celebrated their rites. But what rites?

He drew at his pipe thoughtfully. To think of the Phoenicians was to think of Adonis – that fair youth whose death, burial and resurrection played so marked a role in the solemnities of the Syrian year; whose worship had spread far beyond the bounds of his own land. He was sufficient scholar to be well aware of the importance which the authorities on Comparative Religion had learned of

75

late years to attach to these Nature rituals, traces of which were to be found in all lands. Here in our islands, however, we did not know the *name* of Adonis. That was true; yet all the essentials of the cult had been traced in fragmentary survivals – our seasonal festivals, folk-dances, mumming plays. "Yes, we had the ritual sure enough," he muttered to himself. But where did it come from? Did it grow up spontaneously in different lands, each folk at a given stage of its development having the same conception of a god, ever youthful, ever dying, ever living, on whose beneficent activities all life, vegetable and animal, depended? Or had there been a borrowing? And if there had been contact, and contact on a practically permanent scale, as must have been the case with a foreign community settled on our shore, could there have been anything else?

It was growing dusk now. The traveller re-filled his pipe, lay down on the grass and, his hands clasped behind his head, continued his train of thought.

Supposing the Phoenicians had been settled in this part of the country, was not this just the spot they might have chosen for a temple? He thought of the great temple at Byblos, the centre of the Adonis cult – on the shore looking westward over the sea across whose waves the unfailing current should bring the god from the Egyptian shore. Yes, this was a likely spot for their rites. But of what character would be the worship? Not merely the popular manifestations of sorrow and joy; they would be but an outer part. And here, in a strange land, with but a small public to take part, they would be shorn of much of their importance. No, in a foreign country such as this had been, the cult, restricted to a limited number of worshippers, must have been more personal than public, more esoteric than exoteric in character.

"Of course," he mused, "there was more in the business than these popular rejoicings and lamentations. It wasn't just the spring god, '*la jeunesse éternelle*,' they were worshipping. The old priests and the inner ring knew better than that. What they were after was the ultimate Source of Life. Wonder how far they got? If they got at anything much beyond the physiological facts? After all we have gone little further. Is there more to know? Admitting the possibility of their having known more, what was it? And how did they get at it?"

The night had closed in, soft, fragrant with the aromatic perfume of gorse and heather. From the beach many feet below came the soothing splash and withdrawal of the small waves breaking with idle reiteration at the foot of the cliff. They seemed to say dreamily: "Listen, we are here; but we are doing nothing, neither harm nor good. We are alive, we are strong; but for the moment our life is slumbering, our strength quiescent. We are resting; rest like us." Listening to their distant murmur, at ease on his couch of turf and bracken, the man fell asleep.

But was it sleep that fettered him? This strange sensation of sinking downward, downward into an unfathomable depth of darkness? He was powerless to struggle or cry out. His limbs, his senses were borne down by an unutterable sensation of horror . . . Now he felt firm ground beneath his feet. He was standing upright. But where? In what surroundings? Everything was dark. He dared not move.

Gradually he became conscious of a faint bluish light, or rather of a luminous atmosphere, enabling him dimly to discern his surroundings. He was standing in a small walled space, with columns on either side of him. All was black – floor, walls, the pillar against which he stood, black and cold with a chill that struck to the very depths of his being. Before him, on a black slab raised on a pedestal and approached by steps, lay a still white form behind which burned tapers in tall silver candlesticks, their light seemingly concentrated into two small gleaming points that peered like fiery eyes through the all-pervading haze. Gradually his vision cleared. He grasped what lay before him. It was a dead body, the body of a man, stiff, rigid, with the unmistakable hue of dissolution creeping over it. He had seen dead men before, many times. He had fought as volunteer through a fierce campaign, had seen friend and foe fall around him; yet never had he felt such horror as now lay upon him.

This was not a dead man; it was *Death Itself* – Death in its subtle relentless work of disintegration, going on before his eyes, nay within him. That was the horror. There was something in the place itself, in the environment, which was slowly, relentlessly laying hold of the very springs of his being.

Slowly, slowly, as the grey shadows were creeping over the dead body, so the bitter cold was creeping upward, upward to his heart and brain. He felt his limbs failing and laid his hand for support on the pillar beside him. It was cold, with a chill that struck him to the very heart. Yet he could still *think* dimly. Through the slowly enveloping cold, the awful horror of approaching dissolution, he felt there was something on which he could lay hold, some weapon of defence against this insidious foe. With a tremendous effort he recalled his thoughts from the contemplation of the horror that beset him and bent his energies inward.

Ah! he had it now, the talisman! This that threatened him, threatened the outward form only, not the *I*, the Principle of Life itself; *that* lay deeper, beyond the touch of physical death.

He understood now. Life, true Life, was indestructible. Once called into existence it was and would continue to be. Death, physical death, could lay hold on the body only, the temporary vesture with which Life had clothed itself. Here and now it was still in his power to deny Death that prey.

"*I live!*" The words were uttered at first feebly, then with gaining strength at each reiterated affirmation; till at last his voice rang in a triumphant shout through the vault.

The atmosphere was growing clearer. The strange blue haze was changing colour, becoming suffused with a rosy hue. Over the limbs of the dead man a faint flush was creeping. Was it the flush of returning life? Now the walls around him seemed to fall away; the chapel-vault was widening to a hall. There was light, voices. With a sensation of unutterable relief he knew he was no longer alone. There were men round him in strange garb, with outstretched hands and friendly faces. He gathered he was being welcomed as one long-looked-for and expected, one who had dared and overcome a great danger and reached an appointed goal.

He was entering another hall now, brilliantly lighted, full of folk. One came to meet him in whom he instinctively recognized the host, a tall benign figure, regal, hierarchical, one who might well be both priest and king. He could not tell what words were spoken. It was strange; he seemed to hear no words, and yet to know what was said. He realized that he had passed triumphantly the first stage of a test, a stage beset with grave and terrible danger. He was at a halting-place, a moment of rest and refreshment. There was still more to be achieved. He was conscious of a great lassitude, yet of an underlying tension.

He was seated by his host now at a table. Platters of silver, cups of precious metal, were before them. Up and down the hall moved youths bearing great pitchers from which they poured wine into the cups, filling them to the brim. He set the cup to his lips. The draught ran glowing through his veins, filling him with new vigour. But he was hungry and would fain eat. Where was the food? Why did it delay?

He looked up and met his host's eyes bent on him, calmly, kindly, as one measuring alike his strength and his understanding. Silently he waited. Suddenly there was a stir in the hall. He saw nothing, he heard nothing; yet the atmosphere was vibrant with a force that all seemed to feel. Old men straightened their bent shoulders and sat upright; pallid faces became flushed and rosy; eyes were keen and bright. What had happened? *Something* had passed through the hall – Something that had left behind it an invigorating potency. And behold, the table was no longer bare. Before each man the platter was heaped with viands, strange meats and fruits such as he had never seen, of an odour, a fragrance enticing to the senses.

He looked at his host and felt rather than heard himself put the question: "What passed but now?" He felt also his host's reply, given with a gladness of response: "Thou hast done well to ask, though knowledge is not yet. Eat of the Food of Life!" And he ate, feeling his youth renewed within him.

All languor and weariness had left him now; mind and body were refreshed. All disappointment, all sense of disillusion had vanished like a cloud. He was as one who midway through a long and weary journey should find himself suddenly re-endowed with the vigour and energy, the sense of joyful anticipation, with which he set out upon his course. He ate and drank, and his heart grew light within him.

Suddenly he became conscious that he was alone. Host and fellow-guests had vanished. How or wither he could not tell. He had not seen them pass. The sound of music was in his ears, the scent of flowers was in the air. Now a group of fair maidens surrounded him. He was disrobed by deft hands and led to a couch heaped with soft cushions and silken coverings. He lay down, conscious of a languor that was hardly weariness; for his pulses throbbed with the vigour of youth and through his veins ran the fiery impulse of desire.

His eyes took in the beauty of the attendant maidens – their shining eyes and perfumed hair, their white limbs scarcely veiled by the thin gauze of their robes. He was young and they were fair – and willing. He had but to make his choice.

"See," they whispered, "we await thy will. Time passes. Youth endures but for a short time. Choose now among us. Youth and maiden, we were made the one for the other. *We, we* are the Source of Life. Without us Life would cease to be."

He listened and his senses gave assent to their pleading. Yet even as he did so he was conscious of a questioning within him – of a dim groping after a deeper-lying truth. Before his mind rose the vision of the black chapel and the lifeless body. The horror of his experience was again upon him. What had he learnt then? Surely that beyond and beneath the mystery of physical life lay another and deeper mystery! Slowly, it dawned upon him that, though clothed in so different a form the test confronting him was the same. It was the temptation to rest content with the life of the body – its beginning, its end; to stop short in the quest for the hidden Source of Life itself; to mistake the proximate for the ultimate. He scarce knew what he felt, what were the motives prompting him; but dimly he apprehended that to take what was offered now would be a practical renunciation of the ground already won, a denial of the experience gained. It would be to accept the lower, to reject the higher, solution of the problem. As he had faced the test of bodily dissolution by an affirmation of the indestructibility of Life, so now, before the insistent and insidious claim of the supremacy of bodily Life, he gave utterance to the growing conviction within him: "*I live indeed by the Flesh; yet not by the Flesh alone.*"

And as his mind seized this conviction and his lips affirmed his belief, the music grew fainter, the faces and forms of the maidens receded into the distance . . . He was once more alone.

It was broad daylight now; and again he was one of many. He was clad in white and stood with others in an ordered ring, within the walls of a circular building. Before and behind him, through open doorways, the light and air streamed in, a fresh pungent air laden with the salt tang of the sea, and an aromatic perfume that in some strange way seemed familiar to his sense. In the centre of the vaulted roof was an opening through which the rays of the sun were striking obliquely. He foresaw that very shortly, at midday, the full glory of the light would pour downward . . . on what?

Below this central opening stood a flat stone slab raised on four supporting blocks of masonry. On this, exactly under the opening, stood a vessel, a silver cup in which a spear stood upright. Ceaselessly, from the point of a spear, a thin stream of blood trickled slowly downward into the vessel below.

Behind the altar, facing eastward, stood his host. If before he had seemed to combine in himself the attributes of priest and king, now he was all priest, as in gorgeous broidered robes with filleted hair he stood with folded hands and uplifted eyes awaiting the revelation.

It came slowly, gradually. The point of the spear caught the sunlight, caught and held it. The light spread downward, downward. Now the weapon had changed into a quivering shaft of flame. It was as if the light, flowing downward, were not merely caught and held, but returned upon itself in an upward aspiration. Steadily the illumination grew. The liquid within the cup, suffused with light, swelled upward, a rosy stream on either side of the central flame,

79

overflowing, pouring downward. It was no longer cup and spear, but a glowing Fiery Heart.

"Behold the Flesh transformed by Spirit."

He felt rather than heard the words, all his being intent upon the revelation before him.

Gradually he became aware that the Heart was no mere form, but a quivering, pulsing, centre of Life. Around it the glory grew and spread – a soft rosy glow, quickened as with the beating of countless wings. A ceaseless tremor as of Life pouring downward, soaring upward, spreading outward – spreading, till he felt himself touched with the quickening rays, drawn in towards the glowing centre. He thrilled with a strange poignant bliss, so keen that it was almost agony. Life was pouring into him in every vein, his pulses throbbing with an excess of Life. He was drawing closer, closer, to the very Fount of Life itself. In a very ecstacy of Being it was as if he ceased to be.

With a start the traveller sat upright. It was morning. The sun had risen above the horizon. Below, the wavelets already touched with its beams were breaking idly on the sand. A lark sang shrilly above his head.

He looked round him smiling; then rose to his feet. He was conscious of a strange feeling of refreshment; youth seemed to have returned. Dimly he knew he had passed through some great experience; but what? He could not remember. Had he had a dream? A vision?

He paused, musing. Had he not somewhere read of the practice of Incubation? Of the virtues of the Temple-sleep? These were Temple ruins, he was sure. Was there something in the tradition after all?

With a whimsical smile on his lips he began digging with his stick under a block of stone which lay close to where he had slept. With an effort, using the stick as a level, he raised it to an upright position. *"Beth-El!"* he murmured softly, raising his hat as he turned away.

UPDATE

II

ARTHURIAN LEGEND IN FINE AND APPLIED ART OF THE NINETEENTH AND EARLY TWENTIETH CENTURIES

Roger Simpson

The following items can be added to Christine Poulson's catalogue in *Arthurian Literature*, IX, pp. 81–142.

In preparing this update I have found particularly helpful Charlotte Yeldham's *Women Artists in nineteenth-century France and England*, 2 vols (Garland, 1984). I have also consulted William Fredeman's 'The Last Idyll: Dozing in Avalon' in *The Passing of Arthur*, edited by Christopher Baswell and William Sharpe (Garland, 1988).

I should like to record my gratitude to the Hon. Mrs Roberts, Curator of the Print Room, The Royal Library, Windsor Castle; Dorothy Harding, Curator, Buxton Museum and Art Gallery; Leela Meinertas, Curator, Design Collection, Theatre Museum, London; Richard Jefferies, Curator, The Watts Gallery, Compton; Josian Andrew; Harriet Drummond; Kathleen Morris; and Patrick Mileham.

Dimensions are given in centimetres, height before width.

Abbreviations

A.J.	*Art Journal*
B.I.	British Institution
G.G.	Grosvenor Gallery
M.A.	*Magazine of Art*
N.G.	New Gallery
N.W.S.	New Watercolour Society
O.W.S	Old Watercolour Society
R.A.	Royal Academy
R.A.P.	*Royal Academy Pictures*
R.S A.	Royal Scottish Academy
S.B.A.	Society of British Artists
S.L.A.	Society of Lady Artists
S.M.	Society of Miniaturists

ARCHER, Janet

King Arthur leaving the Nunnery, after seeing Guinevere
S.L.A. 1875

ASHBY, Miss Mabel

Sir Launcelot and Queen Guinevere
N.W.S. 1900

ATKINSON, Maud Tindal

Sir Galahad and the Holy Grail
Watercolour heightened with bodycolour, 74 x 54
Sold Sotheby's 30 July 1974, lot 339
Repr. Sotheby's sale catalogue, as above

BABB, Charlotte E. (fl. 1857–1876)

Queen Iseult
S.L.A. 1876

BACON, John Henry F. (1868–1914)

A Confession of Love:

> Half disarray'd as to her rest, the girl;
> Whom first she kiss'd on either cheek, and then
> On either shining shoulder laid a hand,
> And kept her off and gazed upon her face.

Geraint and Enid

96.5 x 55.9
R.A. 1894
Repr. *R.A.P.*, p. 140

The Passing of Arthur
Signed and dated 1900
Repr. *King Arthur and His Knights*. Stories Old and New (1910), frontis.

BARNARD, Mrs Emily

Arthur in Avillon
S.L.A. 1890

Elaine
S.L.A. 1892

The Beguiling of Merlin
S.L.A. 1897

Guinevere
S.L.A. 1900

BAYNE, Robert Turnhill (1837–1915)

Enid, Geraint and the Earl Doorm. From Tennyson
Design for stained glass for Messrs Heaton, Butler and Bayne.
Repr. *A.J.* (1883), p. 85

BENTON, George Bernard (1872–? fl. 1894–1904)

Three decorative panels:
Geraint in the Lists
The Lady of Shalott
Lancelot
All repr. *Artist* (1902), pp. 67–79

BIRCH, Mrs (Miss Maud Seddon)

Launcelot
N.G. 1899

BLAKE, William (1757–1827)

The Ancient Britons
Watercolour
Exhibited at 28 Broad Street, London, 1809

Merlin
Pencil, 24.6 x 18.8
c. 1819–20
Collection Mr F. Bailey Vanderhoef Jr
Repr. Martin Butlin, *The Paintings and Drawings of William Blake* (1981), cat. 757, plate 986, where it is provisionally identified as 'A Welsh Bard, Job or Moses (?)'. In the Blake-Varley sketchbook (25.4 x 20.3) which was unsold at Christie's on 21 March 1989, leaf 80 recto is a counterproof of Butlin cat. 757, and bears John Varley's inscription 'Merlin': see Robert N. Essick, 'Blake in the Marketplace 1989', *Blake: An Illustrated Quarterly*, 24 (Summer 1990), pp. 221–24 [5–8].

BRICKDALE, Eleanor Fortescue (1872–1945)

Iseult of Brittany
Crayon
Repr. W. Shaw Sparrow ed. *Women Painters of the World* (1905), p. 142

BURLEIGH, Sydney Richmond (1853–1931)

King Arthur Chest
c. 1900
Designed by Sydney Richmond Burleigh
Oak, with Arthurian subjects painted by Burleigh on the panels
Carved by Julia Lippit Mauran
Rhode Island, Museum of Art, R. I. School of Design
Repr. *Ladies of Shalott: A Victorian Masterpiece and Its Contexts* (1985), p. 101

BUTTS, Miss Amy

Elaine
S.L.A. 1868

CARTER, Miss Matilda Austin (1842–? fl. 1862–73)

Elaine: 'And in those days she made a little song / And call'd her song "The song of Love and Death" '
S.L.A. 1868

Elaine:

> Day by day,
> Leaving her household and good father, climb'd
> That eastern tower, and entering barr'd her door,
> Stript off the case, and read the naked shield,
> Now guess'd a hidden meaning in his arms,
> Now made a pretty history to herself
> Of every dint a sword had beaten in it,
> And every scratch a lance had made upon it,
> Conjecturing when and where.

S.L.A. 1868

CLOW, F.

Iseult of Brittany
S.L.A. 1884

COAD, Kathleen E.

Miss Ellen Terry as Guinevere
S.M. 1896

COLLINGWOOD, William (1819–1903)

Tintagel Castle, the Birthplace of Arthur
R.A. 1843

CORBOULD, Edward Henry (1815–1905)

Elaine, the Lily Maid of Astolat
N.W.S. 1861

Morte d'Arthur
N.W.S. 1864
Purchased by Queen Victoria, and presented to Princess Louise

King Arthur's charge to the nuns respecting Guinevere
Watercolour
1865
Her Majesty the Queen

Launcelot's Departure from the Castle of Astolat
N.W.S. 1865

The Contest for the Large Diamond
N.W.S. 1867
Her Majesty the Queen

Pelleas and Ettarre: 'And when they reached Caerleon, etc.'
R.A. 1872

Enid's Dream
N.W.S. 1873

Knight of King Arthur's Court, from Chaucer

CORBOULD, George James (1786–1846)

The Knight and the Hag (from the Wife of Bath's Tale)
R.A. 1802

CRANCH, Christopher Pearse (1813–1892)

The Lady of Shalott
1844

CRIDDLE, Mrs Harry (Miss Mary Ann Alabaster) (1805–1880)

Guinevere and the Little Novice: 'Then to her own sad heart muttered the Queen, /"Will the child kill me with her innocent prate?" '[sic] *Idylls of the King*
O.W.S. 1861

DAVIDSON, Alan

Iseult
S.B.A. 1904

DAVIES, Edgar W. (?–1941)

The Legend of the Sangreal
Cartoon for decoration
S.B.A. 1903

DIXON, Arthur A.

Gareth and Lynette
Sir Lancelot and Elaine
Sir Percival and the Princess
Each is in watercolour heightened with bodycolour, 28.6 x 20.3
Signed
Sold Sotheby's Belgravia 2 November 1971, lot 78

DUNCAN, John McKirdy (1866–1945)

Merlin and the Fairy Queen
Tempera, 63.5 x 53.3
Signed
Renfrew, Art Gallery

FAED, Thomas (1826–1900)

The Lady of Shalott
Collection of John Houldsworth (1860)
Exh. Crystal Palace Picture Gallery (1866)
Sold Christie's 24 March 1866, 4 May 1867, 2 May 1868

FIELDING, Anthony Vandyke Copley (1787–1855)

The Fairy Lake, a scene from La Morte d'Arthur
O.W.S. 1837

FRASER, Miss

Etching from *Idylls of the King*
Amateur Exhibition, 120 Pall Mall, 1860

FUSELI, Henry (1741–1825)

The Knight Finds the Hag Transformed into a Beautiful Young Wife
Oil, 80.8 x 68.6
Petworth House, West Sussex

GARBE, Louis Richard (1875–1957)

The Lady of Shalott
Bronze panel
Arts and Crafts Exhibition, 1903

GIBBS, Henry

King Arthur's Castle, Tintagel
R.A. 1896

GODDARD, Amelia

Elaine: 'And she by tact of love was well aware / That Launcelot knew that she was looking at him'
S.L.A. 1879

GOW, Miss Mary L. (1851–1929)

Enid's Wedding Morning
N.W.S 1875
Elaine
N.W.S. 1876

H., A.

Elaine bearing the shield of Sir Launcelot
S.L.A. 1863

HARTWELL, Charles Leonard (1873–1951)

As he rode down to Camelot
Bronze equestrian statuette
R.A. 1903

HASTINGS, Miss Kate

Guenevere
N.G. 1893

Merlin and Vivian [sic]
N.G. 1895

HEATH, Miss Margaret A.

Elaine
R.A. 1897

HILL, Mrs K.E.

Guinevere
S.B.A. 1898

HOBSON, Mrs Ernest

Elaine
S.L.A. 1887

HODGES, J. Sydney

The Lady of Shalott: 'She saw the water-lily bloom, / She saw the helmet and the plume, / She looked down to Camelot.' – Tennyson
B.I. 1859

Guinevere in the Convent: 'But help me, heaven, for surely I repent, etc' – Idylls of the King
B.I. 1861

HOPE, Robert (1869–1936)

The Passing of Arthur
Signed
Repr. *Highroads of History. Book II: Stories from British History.* The Royal School Series (1935), p. 14

HUGHES, J. Allan (fl. 1886–1928)

Guinevere
Oil, 26.7 x 25.4
Signed
Private collection

HUNT, William (fl. 1894–1900)

The Lady of Shalott
S.B.A. 1896

87

INGRAM, Walter Rowlands (sculptor)

Gyneth: 'Slow the dark-fringed eyelids fall, etc.' Scott's Bridal of Triermain
R.A. 1872

JOY, J.

Queen Guinevere's Dream:

> *Or if she slept, she dreamed*
> *An awful dream, for then she seemed to stand*
> *On some vast plain before a setting sun,*
> *And from the sun there swiftly made at her*
> *A ghastly something, and its shadow flew*
> *Before it till it touch'd her, and she turn'd –*
> *When lo! her own, that broadening from her feet*
> *And blackening, swallowed all the land and in it*
> *Far cities burnt. – vide Tennyson's Idylls of the King*

S.L.A. 1866

K., S.E.

Enid: 'And stood behind and waited on the three' – Idylls of the King
S.L.A. 1864

KEAN, W.R.

Lady of Shalott
Stained glass
Exhibition of Students' Work, South Kensington, 1892

LA FARGE, John (1835–1910)

The Lady of Shalott
Oil, 20.5 x 35.9
c. 1862
New Britain Museum of American Art
Repr. *Ladies of Shalott: A Victorian Masterpiece and Its Contexts* (1985), p. 128

LANGDALE, Marmaduke A. (fl. 1864–1904. d. 1905)

King Arthur's Castle, Tintagel
Oil, 99.1 x 127
R.A. 1866
Repr. *Great paintings in Private Collections*, 2 vols (1905), II, p. 46

LAUDER, Robert Scott (1803–1869)

The Lady of Shalott
National Exhibition, 1854
This is not the work which was exhibited at R.S.A. in 1852

Elaine Tracing Sir Launcelot's History on the Shield
National Institution, 1861

LOUISE, H.R.H. Princess (1848–1939)

Geraint and Enid:

> *Their three gay suits of armour, each on each,*
> *And bound them on their horses, each on each,*
> *And tied the bridle-reins of all the three*
> *Together, and said to her, 'Drive them on*
> *Before you through the wood [sic]'.*
> *He follow'd.*

G.G. 1878

MACBETH-RAEBURN, Henry (b.1859 fl. 1881–1893)

Enid
Etching, after G. Sheridan Knowles
R.A. 1891

MACHELL, Reginald

Parsifal
S.B.A. 1899

MILEHAM, Harry Robert (1873–1957)

Tristram's Deathbed
Oil, 76.2 x 88.9
1902
Exh. Liverpool, Autumn 1902
Sold Whitford and Hughes, *Peintres de l'Ame* exhibition, no. 10, 1984; and
Sotheby's 13 December 1989, lot 181 (on both occasions attributed to Marianne
Stokes)
Private collection
Repr. sales catalogues, as above; and Patrick Mileham, *Characters from English
Literature: Paintings of Harry Mileham FRSA* (an illustrated broadsheet) n.d.

Tristram and Iseult: The Magic Potion
Unfinished oil, 76.2 x 49.4
1900–1905
Exh. Brighton Arts Club, 1951
Private collection
Repr. Mileham, *Characters*

MILLAIS, William Henry (1828–1899)

Elaine, the Lily Maid of Astolat
1862
Coll: William E. Fredeman

MILLER, Felix Martin

Geraint: 'And being ever foremost in the chase, etc.' – Tennyson
Sketch
R.A. 1861

MILLER, William (1796–1882)

King Arthur's Castle, Tintagel
R.S.A. 1877

MOBERLEY, Mrs Maraquita Jenny (née Phillips) (1855–c.1934)

Elaine
S.L.A. 1900

MOGFORD, John (1821–1885)

Vestiges of the Past: King Arthur's Castle, Tintagel
R.A. 1871

MOIRA, Gerald (1867–1959) and Frank Lynn Jenkins (1870–1927)

Scenes from Tennyson's Idylls
Coloured bas reliefs
Trocadero Restaurant, London
The following were reproduced in *M.A.* (1897), pp. 92–97:
*The Coming of Guinevere to Camelot**
Elaine
Enid Bringing up Wine
*Enid Crossing the Drawbridge**
*Hawking**
Hoisting King Arthur's Standard
*Hunting the Wild Boar**
The Queen of the Tourney
The Round Table
Sir Kay the Seneschal
Cartoons for those marked * were reproduced in *Studio* (1897), pp. 227–28
Another set of bas reliefs was made for a library 'in the North of England'. This
set included:
The Lady of Shalott
Merlin and Vivien
Sir Bedivere – the Passing of Arthur

MONOD, Lucien

Study for 'Sir Galahad'
Dowdeswell Gallery
Repr. *Studio* (1904), p. 337

MONTAIGNE, William John (fl. 1839–1889. d. 1902)

*Prince Arthur at the Battle of Caerbadon (He is said to have worsted the Saxons
in twelve successive battles. In one of these, namely that fought at Caerbadon in
Berks, it is asserted that he killed no less than four hundred and forty of the
enemy with his own hand)*
R.A. 1848

MONTALBA, Ellen (fl. 1868–1902)

Elaine
French Gallery, London, 1880

MUNGER, Gilbert

King Arthur's Castle, Tintagel
R.A. 1880

NEWILL, Mary (1860–1947) assisted by Violet and Evelyn Holden

Gareth and Linet
Embroidered panel
Victoria and Albert Museum

Gareth and Lionors
Embroidered panel
Victoria and Albert Museum

NORBURY, Richard (1815–1886)

King Arthur and the Diamond Crown
Liverpool Society of Watercolour Painters, 1874

NORTH, John William (1842–1924)

King Arthur's Pool
O.W.S. 1897

OSBORNE, Miss Emily Mary (b. 1834 fl. 1851–1908)

Elaine
S.B.A. 1865

OSTREHAN, George William (fl. 1893–1903)

Elaine with the shield of Sir Launcelot, talking to her two brothers
Stained glass, 55 x 44.4
Buxton Museum and Art Gallery

PALMER, Samuel (1805–1881)

King Arthur's Castle, Tintagel, Cornwall
O.W.S. 1849

PATON, Sir Joseph Noël (1821–1901)

Rhyme of Sir Launcelot
Sketch
Glasgow, 1854

Sir Lancelot
Oil
c. 1875–1880

PAYNE, Henry Arthur (1868–1940)

Sir Galahad
Design for stained glass
Arts and Crafts Exhibition, 1903
Repr. *Studio* (1903), p. 25

PEABODY, Sophia (1809–1871)

The Lady of Shalott
Sketch
c. 1839

PERCY, Henry S.

The Lady of Shalott
Watercolour, bodycolour, pen and ink
A set of six, each signed, 19.4 x 12.1
Shepherd Gallery (Spring 1983), cat no. 78

PINWELL, George John (1842–1875)

The Lady of Shalott
Watercolour heightened with white, 48.3 x 68.6
Signed
Private collection
Sold Christie's 11 July 1972, lot 157

POCOCK, Isaac (1782–1835)

Nine designs for his *King Arthur and the Knights of the Round Table: A Grand Equestrian Spectacle in three acts.* Drury Lane Theatre, London. 26 December 1834
Pencil and watercolour
Theatre Museum, London

Hall in the Castle of Sir Roland (Act I scene i)
14 x 19

Appearance of Morgana on Serpent, attended by her sprite Ulfo. . .The Horse is led to the Portal (Act I scene i)
13.6 x 18

Castle Rocks in the Valley of St John (Act II scene ii)
19 x 27.7
Nearer View of the Castle Rocks (Act II scene iii)
19 x 27.5

Discovery and Storming of the Castle by the Knights (Act II scene iv)
18.1 x 28

Distant View of the Lists and Tournament (Act III scene iii)
19 x 27.5

The Lists in Preparation for the Tournament (Act III scene iii)
17.8 x 22.2 (inside mount)

The Royal Lists and Tournament (Act III scene iii)
17.8 x 22.2
The Grand Pageant (Act III scene v)
17.3 x 22.2 (inside mount)

POINTER, Myra Drummond

Elaine
S.L.A. 1868

PRIOLAU, Miss E.

How Four Queens Found Sir Launcelot in the Wood
Embroidery, after a design by Jessie M. King
Repr. *Studio* (1910), p. 232

PROUT, Samuel (1783–1852)

Arthur's Castle at Tintagel, Cornwall
R.A. 1808

RANSOM, Frank (sculptor)

The Lady of Shalott
Bust
R.A. 1904

RIVIERE, Briton (1840–1920)

*Elaine: 'The dead, / Steer'd by the dumb, went upwards with the flood.' –
Tennyson*
B.I. 1861

ROPE, Ellen Mary (1855–1934)

A Knight kneeling before the Angel of the Holy Grail
Plaster relief, 91.4 x 62.2
Signed with monogram
Christopher Wood Gallery, November-December 1983
Repr. *Victorian Fanfare*, catalogue of above, plate 1

RUSHTON, George (fl. 1888–1914)

Lancelot
Mural
Repr. J. Hill and W. Midgley, *The History of the Royal Birmingham Society of
Artists* (n.d.), plate 138

SHAW, John Byam Liston (1872–1919)

Sir Galahad
1905
Sir Lanval's Lady appeals to the Judges
Rep. A.R. Hope Moncrieff, *Romance and Legend of Chivalry* (n.d.), p. 224

SHERINGHAM, George (1884–1937)
The Quest of the Holy Grail
Decorative panel
Leicester Galleries, London, 1919
Repr. *Studio* (1919), p. 88

SIDDAL, Elizabeth Eleanor (1829–1862)
The Passing of Arthur (Morte d'Arthur)
Pencil
7.5 x 10 approx.
c. 1855
Private collection
Repr. Jan Marsh, *Elizabeth Siddal 1829–1862: Pre-Raphaelite Artist* (Sheffield, 1991) cat. no. 13

SIMPSON, H.A.
Geraint
Bas-relief
Heatherley Club exhibition at Suffolk Galleries, London, 1893

SLEIGH, Bernard (1872–1954)
Elaine
Tempera
Carfax Gallery, London
Repr. *Studio* (1905), p. 291
The Holy Grail
Oil on board, 49.5 x 59.7
Peter Nahum Ltd, 1989

SMITH, John Coke
The Romance of Sir Tristrem
Mural in Drawing Room at Goodrich Court, Herefordshire (demolished) 1830s
See Thomas Dudley Fosbroke, *The Wye Tour* [c.1842], 65–66; quoted in Clive Wainwright, *The Romantic Interior: The British Collector at Home 1750–1850* (1989), 256.

SPARROW, James
Tristan and Isolde
Stained glass
Repr. *Studio* (1896), p. 112

STEWART, Arthur
The Magic Mantle
S.B.A. 1899
How Sir Bors Rescued a Damsel in Distress
S.B.A. 1900

Sir Galahad
S.B.A. 1900

The Defence of Guenevere
S.B.A. 1902

The Defence of Guenevere
S.B.A. 1907

STRONG, Miss E.F.

Elaine bearing the sleeve-token to Sir Lancelot
S.L.A. 1860

TARRANT, Margaret Winifred (1888-1959)

Elaine in the Barge
Repr. U. Waldo Cutler, *Stories of King Arthur* (1920 edition), p. 184

TAYLOR, Miss Ida R.

The Lily Maid
S.B.A. 1895

TRAQUAIR, Mrs Phoebe Anna (née Moss) (1852–1936)

The Passing of Arthur
Triptych. Enamel on silver. Overall size, including pedestal, 21.6 x 30.5. c. 1905
Nicholas Harris, The Silver and Decorative Arts Gallery, 564 King's Road, London
Repr. *Antique Collector*, 62 (May 1991), p. 58

TURNER, Alfred (1874–1940)

Sir Galahad
Statue
1923
Victoria College, Jersey
Repr. John Christian ed. *The Last Romantics* (1989), fig. 20

UWINS, Thomas (1782–1857)

The Lady of the Lake. From the Romance of Arthur
The Vision of Sir Percivale
Both were included in one frame
O.W.S. 1816

WALKER, Jessica

Merlin and Vivien
Cartoon for stained glass
Repr. *Studio* (1905), p. 351

WATTS,George Frederic (1817–1904)

Enid and Geraint
G.G. 1879 (listed by W.K. West in *G.F. Watts* [1904] but not apparently recorded elsewhere)

WEIGALL, Arthur Howes (fl. 1856–1892)

'There to his proud horse Lancelot turned, etc'
B.I. 1860

WILLIAMSON, F.J.

Elaine
Statue
International Exhibition, 1874
Exhibited in plaster then executed in marble
Repr. *A.J.* (1877), p. 316

WYNFIELD, David Wilkie (1837–1887)

Elaine: 'And she mix'd / Her fancies, etc'. Idylls of the King
B.I. 1860

III

INDEX TO ARTHURIAN LITERATURE
VOLUMES I–X

Compiled by Richard Wright

Arthurian names have been standardised to the commonest forms; cross-references are
only given if the variant spellings are widely separated from the form used. Anonymous
works are listed under title; other works are listed under their author.

A

Aarne-Thompson 5.9
Abbreuiatio Gestorum Regum Franciae 4.2
Abduction 3.27, 29–30, 30–31, 47
Abelard, Peter 6.109
Aberconway abbey 1.70–71
Absalom 8.4
Acallam na Senórach 5.22
Achilles 6.61, 88
Acre 10.28
      siege of 10.30, 31
Acton, John, canon of Lincoln 4.43
Adam 1.118, 137, 146, 151, 152, 159
Adam of Domerham 1.67, 7.110
      on Arthur's burial at Glastonbury 4.37–38, 49, 50, 61, 66;
      Historia de rebus gestis Glastoniensibus 4.47, 61
Adhan 5.83
Adhémar, J. 10.81
Adolf, Helen 8.2–3, 10.32–33, 38, 46, 93
Adventures of Art and the Wooing of Delbchaem 5.21
Adventures of Teigue 5.28
Aelfric 1.56
Aeneas 4.73, 6.61, 94
Aeneid 6.88
Aetius 2.13, 16
Africans, army in Geoffrey of Monmouth 2.11–12, 13, 26, 39
Agag, king 4.159
Aganippus 9.47
Agitius 2.9

29, 41–42, 10.34; burial at Glastonbury 1.66, 77, 4.38, 41, 5.19, 72, 90–91, 6.93–94, 95, 115, 7.109, 111, 112–113, 117, 118, 134; campaign against Romans 2.18–19, 3.39, 41, 4.160–161, 7.17, 18, 9.53; censures Kay 3.16; childhood of 7.35; as chivalric model 7.53; in Chrétien de Troyes 7.56, 65; condemnation by William of Rennes 6.108–109; as conqueror 7.89; continental campaign 7.28; coronation of 2.52–53, 5.138; court of 6.89–92, 8.29–35; his courtesy 9.50–51; death of 1.62–64, 68–69, 68–77, 84–93, 4.37, 42, 149, 152–153, 5.72, 89–91, 6.33, 35, 92–94, 115, 7.114, 118, 8.1, 23; and death of Elaine 2.126; defiance of Roman envoys 3.40; descent from Joseph of Arimathea 4.39; destroys marauding wildcats 5.72, 86–89; downfall of 6.77–78, 7.31, 46, 47, 130–131; engendering of 4.70, 71, 74, 75, 85–90, 6.88, 8.4, 200, 201, 9.29, 39; his epitaphs 1.67–68, 76, 8.103–144; in *Érec et Énide* 1.52–53, 54; establishes kingdom 5.136; evokes loyalty 3.96; exhumation at Glastonbury 1.65–66, 4.45–63, 65–66, 69; fall of 1.118, 163–164; father of Mordred 8.2, 3–4, 6, 9–27, 200, 204; in *Fergus* 8.95, 98, 99, 132, 163, 164, 165, 166, 170; fights giant of St Michael's Mount 4.70, 6.84, 7.73; final conflict with Mordred 1.117, 2.19, 7.116, 143; first meeting with Merlin 5.117; forces assemble for siege of Windsor 1.17–18; forces attack Windsor Castle 1.20–24; and Guinevere 2.117–121, 3.30–31, 97, 7.89–90; and Guinevere's innocence 3.95; Hardyng on 7.118–124, 132, 137, 8.201–203; hears Mordred's accusation of Guinevere 2.120–121; as hero 6.60–61, 63–65, 89, 118–120, 7.55–56, 10.10; in *Historia Brittonum* 6.9, 13–14; historicity of 7.137–138, 139; his hubris 6.64, 70, 71; and hunt for white stag 8.91–94; idealisation 7.98; in Idylls of the King 7.147, 151, 153–155; illegitimacy 7.116; incestuous engendering of Mordred 8.2, 3–4, 6, 9–27; invasion of Ireland 6.49–50, 106; liberation of France 6.106–107; as literary name for Henry II 2.62; in Malory 3.36–37; Merlin prophesies infidelity of Guinevere 2.114–115, 3.37; as one of Nine Worthies 7.105–107; in *Perlesvaus* 1.133; popular and literary hero 6.60–61; reaction to Great Tournament 3.101–103; realm of 1.122–123, 10.47; reign of 7.30–31; return of 1.65–67, 2.31, 4.149, 5.72, 6.93–94, 115, 7.131–132, 142; in *riddarasögur* 7.65–66, 71–74, 100; and the Round Table 2.48, 59–61, 64–65; Scottish attitudes to 8.199–201, 206; self-love 5.96, 122, 129; sends knights on quest 9.77–78; story of 1.95–96; successors 2.10–11, 14, 26, 38–39, 6.33, 35, 7.35; survival 1.62–63, 5.89, 6.94–95, 7.107–108, 131–132, 137; tales of 2.49–50; his tomb 7.108–109, 138–139; in verse romances 7.34–35; visits Brittany 1.13, 14; visits Yvain and Gawain 7.76; in Wace 9.49; wars against Saxons 2.17–18, 4.141, 145, 6.106; William of Rennes' treatment of 6.88–92, 118–120; world of 1.4

Arthur, son of Geoffrey Plantagenet 6.101
Arthur, verse-chronicle 1.70, 76, 7.137, 141
Arthur of Brittany 4.44, 45
Arthur of Little Britain 5.23, 24, 62
Arthur and Merlin 5.79–85
Arthurian legends 6.21–22
    in fine and applied art 9.81–142, 10.111–134; in Latin 1.31–32; narrative material in chivalric discourse 7.51–52; vernacular 6.60–61; Victorian cult of 2.93
Arthurian literature,
    bibliography of 2.127–162, 3.129–136, 4.172, 10.135–160; as ideological literature 2.61–68, 72
Arthurian romances 1.3–4, 2.57, 4.39, 41, 66, 77, 105, 113, 6.89

B

C

107

D

E

F

Gawain   1.7, 25, 2.55, 56, 3.14, 36, 94, 96, 99, 4.77, 5.107, 7.12, 14, 18, 37, 64, 65, 75, 78, 143, 8.26, 31, 33–34, 35, 117, 9.18, 47, 71, 10.34

adventures contrasted with Perceval 10.63–64; adventures in *Diu Crône* 7.31, 38–39, 41, 44–45; arrival at Green Knight's castle 5.13–14; at the Green chapel 5.15–16, 44–57, 60–62; at Hautdesert 5.30–36; axe-blows of Green Knight 5.40, 41–42; betrayal of Pelleas 3.105; birth of 8.10, 11, 17; Chester episode 7.90; in *Conte du Graal* 10.36; contrasted with Kay 7.10, 9.4, 13–14; his courtesy 9.47; crosses into Galloway 10.19–20; death of 6.120; early adventures in *Le Conte du Graal* 10.63–72; in *Fergus* 8.81, 91, 92, 94, 100, 130, 132, 153, 162, 163, 167, 168–170; fight with Lucius 6.79–81, 8.204; fondness for fruit 1.107, 3.49; given Green Girdle 5.37–44; Grail quest 7.31, 45, 47, 10.46; and hunt for white stag 9.73, 76; in *Chevalier de la Charrete* 8.41; his irreconcilability 1.163; journey through wilderness 5.20–28; kills Lamorak 3.95; later adventures in *Conte du Graal* 10.72–88; lost in thought 7.38–39; *Male Pucele* and 3.17, 10.36, 40, 68, 72, 74, 75, 76–79, 85, 86–88; as model knight 2.49, 3.22, 7.53, 10.16; quarrel with Cador 9.53–54; quest for Green Chapel 5.19–29; refuses to defend Guinevere 3.93, 95; rescues Guinevere 7.31; rightful heir to throne 8.200, 201; search for Bleeding lance 10.60–61, 65, 69; sees Green Knight as devil 5.9; selects Alexander as *compaignon* 1.13; sights the Green Knight's castle 5.26–28; son of King Lot 8.1; struck down by Lancelot 3.102; Tintagel episode 10.65–66; in Wace 9.49; welcomes Lancelot to court 8.36–37; and Yvain 2.84–85, 90

Gawain and the Green Knight   see Sir Gawain and the Green Knight
Gaythelos   8.192
Gazoain d'Estrangot   7.34
Geitarlauf   3.78–79, 80, 86, 87
Gellner, Ernest   1.110–113, 117
Genealogia Comitum Flandriae   4.3
Genièvre   *see* Guinevere
Geoffrey of Monmouth   5.16, 6.2, 111, 121, 7.6, 136, 8.23, 185, 193, 201, 206, 9.66, 10.46–47, 86

on the British 6.98–99, 112, 113; death of Arthur 6.95–96; historiography 6.20, 113; *Historia Regum Britanniae* 1.4, 5, 13, 30, 42, 63, 68, 69, 72, 73, 81, 2.50, 59, 99, 100, 3.82–83, 4.41, 48, 5.90, 6.63, 7.17, 21, 28, 51, 59, 91, 101, 114, 133, 8.1, 9.29, 39, 10.17

aim in writing story of Arthur 1.123–124; on Arthur's death 1.63, 65, 69, 7.115; attitude to Gildas 2.22–24; battle of Siesia 6.73, 75, 79–80; Bern manuscript 4.16–26; on Brennius and Bellinus 6.85–86; on Bretons 6.98–99; Christianity in 6.68; comparison with *Gesta regum Britanniae* 6.117–118; conquest of Brittany 6.99–100; considered as appeal for national unity 4.24–25; on Corineus 6.81–85; dedications 4.3, 17–21, 23–9; Gildas as source 2.3–4, 6.27, 28; Leiden manuscript 4.2–6; manuscripts 3.113–28, 4.1–2, 164–171, 5.149–151, 6.159–162, 7.158–162; massacre of the monks of Bangor 6.31, 38–41; mission of St Augustine 6.31, 35–38; parallel passages with *De Excidio Britanniae* 2.4–14, 35–40, 4.155–163; parallel passages with *Historia Ecclesiastica Gentis Anglorum* 6.30–45, 56–59; as political propaganda 7.56; *Prophetiae Merlini* 4.155–157, 6.161–162; on Romans 6.105; Rouen manuscript 4.6–10, 16; on sinfulness of Britons 6.103; sources 10.1, 4–5, 6; treatment of Arthur 6.88, 90, 91, 7.71; use of Bede 6.27–29; Uther and Igerne story 4.70–76, 81, 88, 89–90, 91, 92, 9.35–38; variant version 2.24–30, 4.76, 78, 81, 6.54; verbal reminiscences of *De Excidio*

H

J

K

L

Lynette,
    in Chrétien de Troyes 2.83, 88, 89, 4.85, 7.74, 75, 76, 78; in *Idylls of the King*
    7.150, 155; in Malory 5.11; in modern art 10.127–128
Lyonnel, squire of Lancelot 4.142–144, 145, 147
Lyons, Faith 10.53

M

Mabillon, J. 4.7
Mabinogion 1.134, 7.7, 9.57, 58, 59
Maboagrain 2.85, 3.22, 9.2, 8
McCarthy, T. 3.40
MacNeill, Eoin 6.5–6, 11
Macrobius 10.94
Madden, F. 9.25
Mador la Porte 3.97
Maelgwyn, king of Gwynedd 2.10, 11, 6.17, 23
Magic 1.137, 5.136
    Muslims and 10.79
Maglocunus *see* Maelgwyn of Gwynedd
Magnus Maximus, emperor 6.11, 30, 32
Magnús V Erlingsson, king of Norway 7.67–68
Magnús VI Hákonarson, king of Norway 7.59, 69
Maid of Astolat 3.92, 92–93, 97–101, 101, 103, 7.144
Maiden Castle 8.136
Maihew, Edward 4.67
Mainistrech, Flann 6.6
Major, John 7.117
Malatesta, Rambetus 10.1–2
Malcolm III Canmore, king of Scots 8.189
Malcolm IV, 'the Maiden', King of Scots 1.31
Malduc 5.58
Male Pucele 3.16, 17, 10.36, 40, 68, 72, 74, 75, 76–79, 85
Malgo 6.33
Malory, Sir Thomas 1.122, 125, 128, 131, 156, 157, 163, 2.70, 97, 98, 99, 101, 3.34,
    88, 5.11, 32, 91, 95, 122, 126, 6.97, 7.21, 92, 8.2, 16, 17, 20, 25, 186, 191
    access to sources 4.95, 101, 105–108, 122, 125; archaic mind 1.110–120;
    consciousness of modernity 195; and death of Arthur 1.68, 74–77, 7.103–144;
    identification 4.95–96; implicit attitudes in 1.102–110; on Lancelot 3.35–52,
    4.114–118; moral earnestness of 1.102–105; nostalgia in 1.119; patronage 4.94,
    108–109, 118; possible connection with Anthony Wydville 4.95–96, 111–112; as
    source for Soseki 2.94, 96–97; sources 3.35–36, 7.103–104, 137; style
    1.99–102; as traditional writer 1.94–99
    Le Morte Darthur
      'Book of King Arthur' 9.76–78; 'The Book of Sir Launcelot and Queen
      Guinevere' 3.91–112; 'The Book of Sir Tristram de Lyones' 3.92, 95; Caxton
      and 4.108–110, 5.91, 7.137–138; compression in 1.98–99; enchantment in
      1.99; Grail Quest 1.128–131; hunt with a white bratchet in 9.76–78, 79, 80;

N

P

S

T

U

V

149

W

Y

Yvain   3.14, 24, 4.85, 7.35, 38, 41, 45, 48, 63, 65, 8.117, 10.33–34, 49
    Chester episode   7.90; as *Chévalier au Lion*   2.88–91, 3.14; chivalry   7.55;
    encounter with lion 9.4; as exemplary figure   7.89; in *Fergus*   8.81, 91, 163; as
    fin amant   2.79–85; forgets to return from the tourney   2.85–86, 3.18–19, 21,
    7.64, 75; madness of   3.19, 20; makes chivalric reputation 3.19, 20, 21; as model
    knight   7.53; in *riddarasögur*   7.75–80
Yvain of the White Hands   7.15–16
Yvain   see Chrétien de Troyes, *Chévalier au Lion*
Ywain and Gawain   5.25, 29, 7.79, 89–90, 98

Z

Zaddy, Z.P.   9.1–2, 15, 16, 17, 20
Zifar   7.97
Zimmer, Heinrich   5.7–8

Contents of previous volumes